Gordon Lewis

Secret To Sultan

The follow on book to *Secret* Child

The boy grows up and follows his dreams

Copyright © 2020 Gordon Lewis All rights reserved

No part of this book may be reproduced, or stored in a retrieval system, or transmitted in any form or by any means, electronic, mechanical, photocopying, recording, or otherwise, without express written permission of the publisher.

ISBN-13: 9798689594071

Cover design by Tannishtha Chakraborty
tannishtha.chakraborty@gmail.com

Chapter One

The Deal

I awoke, as usual, to the sound of my alarm clock. With the warmth of the sun shining into my bedroom, it felt as if life couldn't be much sweeter. It certainly didn't feel like today would be etched on my memory for all the wrong reasons, but simply just another day of working long hours in a job I truly loved. The forecast on the radio was for another hot summer's day, which was to be expected as London was in the midst of a heatwave. I moved around my new house drinking countless cups of tea, much to do with my Irish upbringing. I left the house without breakfast, knowing it would be served at work; just one of the perks of my job. My boss was a demanding and impatient man; a well-known television director. He would expect me and the television crew to be at the north London location with the cameras ready and in position before he arrived.

I was young, and my mind was in constant overdrive. If you didn't know me, you might think I was a little hyperactive at times. But who could blame me? I was in the world of entertainment, meeting and working with famous people. However, I did have one big regret. I hadn't spent as much time with my mother and stepfather as I would've liked. Cathleen and Bill were very understanding and never made any fuss about it. Still, I felt terrible for not visiting more often. Deep down, I knew the phone calls were never as good as seeing them face to face.

'Don't worry about us; you're doing exactly what you've always wanted to do. Things don't just happen y'know, you have to work hard to succeed in show business.' Mum would always tell me this when I visited her in the little free time I had. With these constant reminders and encouragements all my life, Mum had made me determined and self-sufficient from a very early age. The mindset she taught me was probably a necessity for her own survival, rising from the difficult situation she found herself in having me out of wedlock in 1950s Ireland. Despite having to keep me a secret from the world for nine years, my mum led by example to instil a very good work ethic in me. Somehow she always made me see sense when I needed it most. Mum took a keen interest in the showbiz personalities I was working with and constantly asked me about them like they were old friends. It was as if she had met them, but all her information came from newspapers or the television and occasionally, me. It was her way of staying close to me, which I found both comical and delightful at times.

Mum never looked her age and was always young at heart. Her piercing blue eyes, which I inherited, made her a very attractive and engaging person. Having me late in her life meant it was quite a struggle to bring me up, and being a single mother in the 1950s was a real taboo in Ireland. On top of that, I was very boisterous and always pushing my luck. I really was quite the little devil and not at all easy to control; I put it all down to my unusual circumstances. To her credit, my mum was incredibly patient with me. She was relentlessly positive and believed that anything was possible if you only try. Even though I saw little of Mum in my younger years because she worked full time in Dublin, our relationship was a close one and we had a deep understanding of one another. There was only one thing we did disagree on.

After working in the entertainment world for several years, I had already seen many people with addictions. She was addicted to her beloved cigarettes. When she knew I was coming to visit, Mum would open all the windows and get out the air freshener to cover up the traces of her smoking.

'Ah, I smell the air freshener again. How many have you had today?' I enquired, only half playfully.

'Oh, stop it – you cheeky little devil! I have this one vice, my only indulgence. Can't you let me have that?' She made a face of disapproval.

'I'm just saying, it's not good for you, Mum. Only because I care about your health.'

'I know you care, but don't worry about me. I'll be fine. Have you had anything to eat? I have a lovely Irish stew in the pot…'

My mum knew just how to change the subject of a conversation when she needed, and she knew the way to my heart was food. I loved Mum's cooking and had really missed her food since moving into my new house.

Bill, my stepfather, was much older than my mum. But with relentless effort and energy, I kept him young. He had worked as a master carpenter in the film industry since arriving in London from Dublin in the 1950s, and later worked in the theatres, building sets and scenery for the live shows. When Mum and I came to London to join Bill, he couldn't work me out; it wasn't for want of trying. Looking back, it took time for him to get to know me. It must have been tough for Bill to adapt to the new responsibility of being a husband and a father all at once. Before Mum and I arrived from Ireland, Bill was your typical Irishman and a happy-go-lucky bachelor. I wasn't sure about him to begin with. Who is this man who's getting a share of my mother's love and affection, I found myself wondering. However, his patience and gentle ways finally found a way with me. Bill also got used to my ways eventually. As the years quickly passed, I learnt to trust and love this good, kind man who did the best he knew how for the woman he loved – my mum.

Bill was looking forward to taking life easy with his recent retirement but Mum had other ideas.

'Bill Lewis,' she said, 'are you going to spend all your free time in the pubs now, are you?'

'Yes, my dear. I've just retired having spent over fifty-one long years working. Can't I have some time to relax for a little while, please?'

'Sure, have some time to rest, but there's plenty of jobs that need doing around the house. The sooner you get them done, the better. Or perhaps I should retire too and let you do all the cooking and cleaning from now on?' Mum replied.

'Soon enough, Cathleen. I'll get round to them! I'm taking Brandy for his walk now, he knows it's time.'

'Stopping off at the pub on the way?'

'Just for a quick pint on my way back,' he admitted.

Mum knew all of Bill's habits and ways. Like a lot of Irishmen, he cherished the atmosphere of the pub. He was no saint but he was an honest and compassionate man. Knowing Mum, I was sure she would find a way to keep him busy in his retirement years.

On that hot sunny morning, as I arrived at the Rainbow Theatre in north London, I only had the day ahead of me on my mind. The theatre was now a live music venue, and as I walked through the doors, memories from years ago came flooding back. I was greeted by a friendly stage doorman who offered to show me around. The truth was, I already knew the place inside out. I used to visit the Rainbow Theatre religiously with my best friends Gerard and Brian Greene every Saturday morning to watch the black and white Batman films. I would pay to get into the theatre and then let my friends in through one of the side doors, collecting the money from them myself. Nothing much had changed over the years, except for the addition of some more bars around the venue. Alcohol had replaced ice creams.

Around the corner, in Finsbury Park, was the laundry shop where Mum worked as the manager when we lived in that area. Life was not easy for immigrant families looking to rent rooms, with signs in shop windows saying 'No Irish, no Blacks, no dogs'.

I'll never forget the day I received two free tickets from one of Mum's best customers to see The Beatles live on stage in the same theatre I now found myself working in.

The tickets were like gold dust; I could have sold them for a lot of money. But seeing The Beetles was not an opportunity I wanted to miss. Bill decided that I was far too young to go on my own and was going to accompany me.

'Are you sure you want to go to the concert?' Mum asked him. 'You're always complaining about The Beatles and their long hair. You say they can't sing and you're forever comparing them to The Bachelors from Ireland. Don't you think Gordon might like to take a friend with him instead?'

Secretly, I think Bill did want to see The Beatles, if for no other reason, just to see what all the fuss was about. When we arrived at the theatre, every seat was taken. When they finally came on stage, much later than expected, everybody went wild with excitement. The teenage girls in front of us stood up and started screaming.

'Girls! Girls! Please sit down! You're blocking the stage! And stop shouting,' Bill exclaimed. He was completely ignored, of course, and soon he was holding his hands over his ears. I joined the crowd and started shouting, standing on the seat to see the band.

'All this noise! It's not music! Are you enjoying this, Gordon?'

I ignored him and continued shouting and singing along while standing up on the seat. Bill got up after the second song and spent the rest of the evening in the theatre bar. As for me, I was loving every minute. The whole atmosphere was electric and I knew, from that night, this was the world I wanted to be part of one day.

The television crew soon turned up in their numerous vehicles and began unloading equipment ready for the day. The catering truck was already serving breakfast. Soon the heavy cameras were lifted into their positions to capture the stage performance. The client for this video shoot was AWB – Average White Band. They wanted three live music videos for the marketing of their new album. Like a lot of bands and artists they arrived late, which was quite normal in the rock and roll world. However this meant I was already getting behind schedule. Sometimes you can easily make up the lost time, if you're lucky. But luck was not on my side today. As the producer, I would need to have a chat with the dubious theatre guy and ask for extra time, however he wasn't particularly easy to track down.

We were working on the last song, 'Let's Go Round Again'; the television crew were into the music, tapping their feet to the song. The playback was extremely loud with the band miming to the song. Just then, my runner came up to me and informed me that Bill was on the telephone wanting to speak with me.

'Can you tell Bill I'm dealing with a problem and I'll

call him back later? Thanks.' The runner went off.

The theatre guy appeared at last and I told him I would need an extension to finish the last song. He wasn't particularly eager to agree and wanted to close the venue at the time we previously agreed. I had to try and use some magic on him, which was all part of my job. I asked him to walk with me to the top floor bar for a beer, knowing he probably wanted some cash in hand to allow us to overrun and finish the shoot that night. His attitude changed when the cash was handed over and I was pleased to have secured some extra time. My runner returned, sprinting up to me at speed. He was gasping for air and I could tell something was wrong.

'Gordon, I was looking for you, Bill is still holding on the phone. He said it's urgent and that he's at the hospital!'

I was shocked and immediately rushed to the phone at the stage door.

'Hi, Bill, what's wrong?'

'Sorry Gordon, didn't mean to take you away from your work but your mum is in the local Tottenham hospital.' Bill explained in his usual calm way. He was never one to panic.

'Is she okay, Bill? What's wrong? Did she have an accident?' My mind and heart were racing.

'No, not an accident. I'm not sure what the problem

is, Gordon. She kept falling into this deep sleep, on and off. It got me worried so I called the doctor. After he examined her, he asked that I take her to the hospital.'

Bill tried to reassure me she was in good hands with the doctors and nurses. I wasn't totally convinced, though. I couldn't understand how this was happening; Mum was always healthy. The last time she'd been to hospital was to have me, 23 years ago.

'Gordon, you can't do anything for her at the moment – she's asleep. Come when you finish work, I'll be here at the hospital waiting for you.'

'Okay, I'll be there as soon as I can,' I said.

The last time I was in a hospital was in Dublin when I was six. I needed to have my tonsils out and it's safe to say I didn't enjoy the experience. Mum could only come to visit me in the evenings after work and she'd sit and talk with me while playing with my hair. Before my tonsils were taken out, she promised me a new cowboy outfit if I was a good, brave boy. A few days later, I walked out the hospital with my new cowboy hat and gun. Mum always knew how to deal with me; she could read me like a book at that time.

Mum came from an Irish generation who were suspicious of hospitals, believing you either came out alive or died in there. Walking into the hospital later and looking for Mum's ward, I felt an icy apprehension in the pit of my stomach. I wasn't sure what to expect. I kept thinking about Mum's doubting words, 'alive or dead'. They played on my mind, repeating over and over like a broken record. Usually I would have gone out for dinner and a drink after a production 'wrap'. But the last thing on my mind that night was food. I found Bill sitting beside Mum's bed where she was sleeping. He looked dapper and smart in his customary suit and tie, but a look of concern hung on his face.

'How's Mum? What did the doctor say?' I asked, apprehensively.

'Oh, there you are. She's okay, I think. All the doctor said was that they'd carry out some tests over the next couple of days and let us know. Pull up a chair, Gordon, she's been asleep for the last few hours.'

'It's okay, Bill, I prefer to stand,' I replied.

I was restless and paced a few steps, trying to shift the nervous tension knotting itself in my stomach. I didn't know what was wrong and I couldn't do anything for her. The insufferable feeling of helplessness was eating away at me already. This was another side to my nature; I like to be in control. After about twenty minutes, a nurse suggested we leave as it was late. She assured us Mum was in good hands so I decided to invite Bill to have a night-cap at the pub near the hospital. I knew a drink would go down well with him that evening.

It was after a few drinks when Bill revealed that Mum had not been her best for a while, but she had insisted that he did not mention anything to me.

'She didn't want to make any fuss over her appetite and the weight loss. She didn't want you to be worrying about her,' Bill admitted.

I was completely taken aback with what Bill told me. I had thought of myself as a relatively insightful and perceptive person until that moment. However, the true extent to which I had been wrapped up in my own dreams was now becoming apparent.

'Your mum always looks forward to seeing you, Gordon, she's so proud of how well you're doing. She knows you love your work and that you need to spend a lot of time there.'

Even with Bill's reassurances, I felt guilty listening to him talk about Mum. He lit another cigarette.

'I should've said something when she started losing weight. I saw it but I didn't ask. I didn't think much of it,' I said, feeling completely lost.

'I didn't think much of it either at first. Not until she started feeling weak and falling asleep in the chair. She's usually so energetic,' said Bill. 'You know it's not in her nature to complain.'

I began to realise Mum had been putting on a show of normality for me and making Bill play along with the masquerade.

Days turned into weeks in the hospital and the doctors were still trying to find out what was wrong with Mum. She was still losing weight and rather weak. Bill and I were becoming more and more distraught at the fact they hadn't diagnosed the problem. Our lives had been turned upside down; Mum was the glue at the heart of our family. One evening I arrived at the hospital and a doctor asked to speak with me. He said they believed that a prescription prescribed by my mum's general practitioner had been the cause of her problem. Bill and Mum lived in Broadwater Farm in Tottenham, one of the biggest council estates in the country. She was chased one evening after work and the incident had caused anxiety for which Mum was prescribed some medication. After the hospital diagnosis, and a change in prescription, we could see a turning point in her recovery.

'I can't wait to get Cathleen out of this place, Gordon. It's really miserable in here, you know. The smell of antiseptic is a constant reminder of death and disease. And the food is awful,' Bill said. 'Not that she's eating much anyway,' he added.

'With some luck, she'll be out of here in a few days,' I replied, feeling confidant at last.

I had spoken too soon. Two days later, she developed pneumonia and had fluid in her lungs. I had always known Mum to be a fighter with an unrelenting positive attitude. Although we were presumably feeling the same devastation, I did not disclose my feelings to Bill. Mum started refusing to eat and we both felt as if she was beginning to give up. Seeing her lying in the hospital bed was a wakeup call to the inevitability of mortality and that it was only a matter of time until her life came to an end.

The next morning, I was in the hospital again with Bill trying to reassure me.

'She'll be fine, you'll see. Don't worry, Gordon.'

I appreciated his efforts but as we stood by the bedside, I couldn't help thinking the worst. My mind drifted to wondering how Bill would cope without Mum in his life. The doctors had asked Bill to remain by Mum's bedside and keep talking to her. He was very committed and did this religiously each day. But still Mum remained in a strange deep sleep without any real movement except for the rise and fall of her chest. Bill would arrive at the hospital early in the morning and stay until the evening. He would talk about all the enjoyable things they had done in their time together. With all his heart, he did not want to let her go. It was very distressing and painful for me to watch.

'I was thinking about building that new kitchen area you always wanted – to make room for all the jars of jam you'll make this year. When you're better, we'll look to have a lovely holiday somewhere nice,' Bill would say, gently holding and stroking her hand, never taking his eyes from her even for a second. It seemed as if he was trying to create something eternal between them.

I was ringing the office every few hours from the public telephone within the hospital, using small bags of change. My boss was understanding but he relied on me solely to deal with artist management and the record company people, who could be crazier than the artists they represented. My sleep was fitful as I didn't want to miss anything and I lived in constant fear of what might happen next. I found myself frequently visited by nightmares and would wake up anticipating the words, 'She's gone'. But still I couldn't bring myself to discuss this with Bill.

One evening, almost a week after her pneumonia, Bill and I were getting ready to leave the hospital. Just as Bill was telling Mum that we'd be back in the morning, she opened her eyes. In that moment she looked happy; some semblance of her old self for the first time in forever. She didn't say anything, only smiled. Bill moved up close and kissed her. I was momentarily overjoyed but my fractured nerves quickly took hold and I thought, could this be it? Is this how it'll end? But then, to my happy astonishment, she said 'Any chance of a cup of tea?' We laughed; of course the first drink she asked for was tea, not water. I saw this as a good omen.

I rushed to inform the nurse and then got her the cup of tea. A sort of nervous relief descended upon Bill and I, but we weren't sure how long this would last.

Over the next few days, the senior hospital consultant wanted to do a few more tests as he was still unsure of Mums condition. She was making slow progress. Bill always had the telephone number of wherever I was working, just in case he needed to call me. Mum was lucky to have friends and family who came to see her. She was very well-liked and appreciated. Her nephew, Dennis, and his wife, Nellie, would make her laugh, offering to place bets on horseraces for her. She grew up with horses in Ireland and they shared the excitement of the races. Other family members came over from Ireland to see her, perhaps fearing the worst.

'I've had enough of hospitals, Gordon. Please take me home. Tell the doctors I want to go home,' she asked, almost pleading with me.

'We want you home, Mum, but we have to see what the results of the tests are first. I heard Nellie and Dennis were here again earlier today.'

'Yes, they were. It's kind of them to visit so often.' Mum paused. 'The truth is, I don't really want people to see me like this; I'm embarrassed. I look a mess, I'm so frail. It's awful, Gordon.' Her weak voice choked as she spoke and I felt my own throat tighten.

'Please talk to the doctors. They'll listen to you. Just let me go home,' she continued. I was beginning to well up and I didn't trust myself to speak so I just hugged her.

'I'll speak to the doctor, okay?' I whispered, knowing that she wouldn't be able to leave the hospital any time soon.

Bill pulled me aside and told me that Mum was still putting on her best show for me, and that she'd been really down; completely uninterested in visitors and food. The only time she would look at herself using the small mirror was when she knew I was on my way.

'I'm going to look for the consultant doctor to discuss Mum's situation,' I told Bill while trying to swallow my rising anxiety. I was still putting on a brave face for them both. A nurse came up to me unexpectedly and asked if Bill and I could join her to see the doctor in his small white room.

'I'll come to the point, gentlemen. We've looked at the x-ray of Mrs Lewis's lungs and I'm sorry, but I don't have good news for you,' the doctor said, matter-of-factly. My heart sank as I looked across at Bill, who was looking equally as worried. The doctor put the x-ray on the lightbox and pointed.

'We've noticed her loss of interest in people and her

surroundings. Mrs Lewis is probably suffering from depression due to the length of her stay in hospital. All of this hasn't helped, but we need to work fast to operate and remove the cancer.' The word cancer came as a complete surprise.

'You said cancer' I said, not quite believing what the doctor was telling us.

'Yes.' He paused. 'We will have to remove one half of her lung to make sure it doesn't spread.'

'She will survive?' I asked, tentatively.

'She has a good chance of surviving the operation itself, though her weak health does add additional risk. As for the cancer, that's another matter.'

'But you can help her, right?' Bill butted in. The doctor paused and looked at me before he replied.

'Yes, we'll do our best, but her life will be limited as the cancer looks aggressive.' I sensed that the doctor was preparing us for the worst.

'How long are we looking at?' I asked, dreading what may follow.

'Could be as much as one year. Perhaps a little longer, with some luck.' There was an awful silence. Bill and I didn't know what to say.

The doctor broke the silence, insisting that we consent to the operation now so that it would be rushed through the next day.

'Would you prefer to inform Mrs Lewis, or do you wish me to discuss the cancer and operation with her?' the doctor asked, looking at me. This felt unreal.

'I'll talk to my mother about it. Leave it to us, please,' I said after a moment of pulling myself together in the wake of the shock the doctor had delivered.

We walked out of the office, back to Mum's bedside, in a daze. We were unable to speak. As I saw her looking tired and dejected, I made an extra effort to compose myself and be strong, as she had been for all these years. I told her she would be having an operation tomorrow in the same manner you might tell someone they are going to have their hair cut. I did not mention anything about her cancer.

I asked Bill to join me in the pub; we needed more than a stiff drink that evening, for sure. As we sat down in Bill's regular corner of the pub, he pulled two tablets out of his jacket pocket and then took them with his Guinness. The poor man was on medication to cope with the stress he had been under for months. I had been relying on alcohol to relax after work. Bill looked at me and asked the question I'd been expecting since we left the hospital.

'How and when will you tell our Cathleen?' His face was ashen with concern.

I chose my words carefully. 'Bill, I'm going to have to ask you to trust me on this.' I was trying to bring back some of my usual positive and up-beat self. 'Can you promise me you won't tell Mum she has cancer? We can call it the 'C' word between us.'

He hesitated in a kind of bewilderment. 'What are you talking about, surely we have to let her know.' I could tell Bill was very uncertain. 'Sorry, Gordon, I'm not sure this is the right thing to do.'

'Bill, trust me. If we tell her she has cancer, she'll just give up. No offence, but I know my mum better than anyone in the world.'

He stared thoughtfully into his pint and then took another big gulp of the black nectar. In the minutes of silence that followed, Bill lit up his fourth cigarette. He was chain-smoking.

'How are you going to tell her about the shortening of her life without mentioning the 'C' word?'

'I don't know yet. Give me until tomorrow night to think about it. Please don't ask me anymore questions, Bill. I just want to keep her alive, to extend her time with us.'

We spoke very little about it for the rest of the evening. As I put Bill in a black cab later on, he asked me if I was sure what I was doing. I tried to hide my unsettled mind with a weary smile and nodded to reassure him.

When I got home, I did something I don't normally do. I opened a bottle of red wine to drink on my own.

I wasn't ready for bed; my mind was still processing the events of the last 24 hours, the last week. The last few months. The television was on in the background, helping to drown some of the relentless noise inside my brain. I was on my second glass already, knowing I would drink the whole bottle before going to sleep. All I could think of were the memories of me and Mum in Dublin, and arriving in London to live with Bill. I found myself taking out photos of me with them both when I was a teenager. Happy memories of the past were quickly overwhelmed by guilt. I'd been taking Mum for granted for too long, and with the deterioration of her health came a nauseating realisation: loss was very real and terribly permanent. I kept thinking I should have done more for her; my wakeup call had seemed to come too late. The house phone started ringing; it was past midnight. It could only be the hospital calling at this time. Once again, I braced myself for the worst and picked up the phone.

'Sorry to be ringing you so late. Did I wake you up?' It was Bill.

'No, it's okay. I'm up. Are you alright?' I spoke as soberly as I could.

'I need to talk to you. I hope you understand,' he stammered. 'I can't sleep.'

'It's alright, Bill. I can't sleep either.'

There was a pause from Bill, and then he just broke down and began to cry. I tried so hard to comfort him and reassure him that something good would come out of this, without crying myself. I had to be strong for him.

'I'm so sorry Gordon. I just can't believe what's happening, and what's going to happen to Cathleen…'

It was more comfortable to talk on the phone that night, for some reason. But I could tell he was on the hard stuff, probably brandy.

'What are you drinking?' I asked, pouring my third glass of red wine, searching for some kind of emotional comfort. I was not great at expressing my real emotions. I let Bill talk about the old times and what a great woman Mum was to us both. I was welling up too. He reminded me of all the beautiful things she did for me and how much he loved her. When we had finished talking and I put the phone down, my emotions finally got the better of me. For the first time since this nightmare began, I found myself crying uncontrollably. I was just relieved nobody was around to see. There is so much pride in me and I never let things get the better of me. But the idea of losing Mum was just too painful to comprehend and there was simply nothing I could do.

Pouring the last glass of wine from the bottle, I decided to do something I never thought I'd do. I was raised as a Catholic until, at the age of thirteen, I lost my faith in the church and decided I didn't need religion anymore. But there I was kneeling on my red carpet floor, making the sign of the cross like a faithful Catholic.

'God, I'm really not good at this. I don't go to Mass and I don't believe in the Catholic Church. But if you are there, I need your help. Please forgive me for what I am about to ask but I believe only your help can allow my mother to live for many years to come. Can we do a deal? Sorry, I told you I'm not good at this. If you let Mum live, I will try so hard to be a better person; I might just surprise you.'

I blessed myself, got up off the floor and I drank the last drop of red wine. I was now smashed. The next morning I awoke dehydrated with a hangover. But I remembered everything from the night before and my deal with God.

Chapter Two

The Unfortunates

Looking back on my early years, growing up in Dublin, I was always a happy child with not a care in the world. My mammy, as I would call her when we lived in Ireland, would always say, 'you are blessed, you little rascal,' while tickling me, causing me to break out in laughter. After the lengths she had gone to just to keep me in this world, we were naturally close. I meant everything to her; I was her secret. By the law of averages, I was already ahead in the game of life just to be here. Mammy worked long hours, six and a half days a week. It wasn't easy to keep me a secret from her family and the rest of the world.

My home on the north side of Dublin was not what you might call a conventional home. We lived in Regina Coeli: a large overcrowded hostel for single mothers. It was the late fifties and neither the conservative Catholic Church nor Irish society were very sympathetic towards unmarried mothers. Discreetly sending children away from Ireland for adoption was generally the Irish solution to the issue, with the Church receiving money for each child.

I grew accustomed to being called names, some funny and some not so amusing. I didn't mind being known as one of the local 'unfortunates'. But, as you would be able to tell by the bloody nose I gave you, I didn't like being called a bastard.

'He has the luck of the Irish; he can't go wrong!' my friends would say. This was more related to my ability for getting into mischief without being caught, rather than my good fortune.

Away from school, I loved nothing more than exploring the streets of Dublin, wild and unrestrained. I was the youngest of a small group of 'unfortunates' from the hostel who would wreak havoc at every opportunity. All in the name of fun, of course. We were menacing looking boys, jumping on and off moving buses without paying the fares. We may not have had any money but that certainly wasn't going to stop us embarking on an epic adventure!

School was very basic in the early 1960s and I had great difficulty learning to read. Not that my school had many books to read anyway. It wasn't until much later on, when I still struggled to read and write, that people began to notice. There was nothing in the way of diagnosis or support for dyslexic children at this point; my attention span was short and I was always full of energy. I wasn't exactly a model student and spent each day simply waiting for the school bell to release me from boredom. But what I lacked in the classroom, I made up for in street smart. There was only one subject I was perceived to be any good at: religious studies. To me the Bible stories sounded like magic, which I found fascinating. The priests, known to us children as 'the men in black', did a fantastic job of instilling the fear of God into me.

'You will go to hell if you aren't good children. Did you say your prayers last night and this morning before you went to school?' Before we knew it, we were praying again.

At the age of thirty-five, my mother fell in love with a charming Catholic businessman called John Sullivan. John loved her in return but he was not completely honest. Over time, my mother became suspicious that the man she loved was hiding something. However, this was a time when women didn't question men so she said nothing. The secret was only confirmed when she gave him the news of my impending arrival. John finally came clean about his wife and family in Cork. He did not want anything to do with me.

'Why not go to London and have an abortion? I'll organise and pay for everything,' he said. My mammy was devastated.

It was illegal in Ireland to have an abortion, and keeping a child out of wedlock wasn't looked kindly upon either. But Mammy was a free-thinker and decided to have me on her own, despite knowing there would have to be sacrifices. John Sullivan disappeared suddenly so Mammy engaged a Jewish lawyer to find him and threaten him into paying something towards the upkeep of his child. The case was set to go to the Children's Court in Dublin, but at the last minute it was settled out of court. A one-off payment of three hundred Irish pounds for the baby with no reference to the father's name on the birth certificate. Because it was a 'no win, no fee' basis, Mammy received £150 of this. The papers were signed and they never saw each other again.

Mammy was fortunate to find Regina Coeli, a safe haven away from prying eyes. Irish society did not acknowledge such a place could exist. It was a community of over one hundred single mothers and their children, living in open dormitories. Each dormitory had rows of beds and an open fire for warmth and cooking. There was very little privacy, living in such close proximity to one another, which inevitably lead to some arguments and occasionally fights between the mothers. The children were provided one free meal each day. All the mothers had to contribute to the upkeep of the hostel but they were happy just to have a roof over their heads. It was a safe place, hidden away from judgement, sandwiched between the mental institution on one side and the men's hostel on the other.

Mammy worked as a waitress in a hotel in the city centre of Dublin until the time I was born Francis Gordon McCrea, on 25 February 1953. She had changed her surname by adding 'Mc' in front of 'Crea' and lived a secret double life from then on. She didn't tell her family and friends anything of her new life or her secret child. This continued for almost nine years until I became a problem with the Garda, the Irish police.

With my unquenchable appetite to explore the world outside the walls of the Regina Coeli, I inevitably got picked up by the Garda. I would arrive back at the hostel in style, in the police car. It happened again and again as I thought Mammy would never find out. When she finally found out, she did what all mothers did at that time; she gave me a real good hiding.

'I won't do it again, Mammy. I promise!' I shouted as I ran around the table in the dormitory.

'I am so disappointed with you, Gordon!' she

exclaimed, whacking me with her hand on my bottom when she caught up with me.

I broke away from her hold and screamed at the top of my voice, 'You are never here. Never!'

She stopped in her tracks and started to cry, kneeling down with her hands on her face sobbing. I stopped crying and ran to hold her.

'I'm sorry, Mammy. I won't do it again. I'll be a good boy from now on.' She held me tight and kissed me on the cheeks.

'I'm so sorry. I know I work a lot of the time but it's all for you, Gordon. I wish I could be here for you more but it's just not as easy as that. I won't hit you again, I promise'.

That night, after putting me to bed and waiting until everyone else was asleep, she spoke to Bridie – another single mother in the hostel who was a close friend and confidant. I pretended to be asleep but I was listening with keenness.

'Gordon's out of control. I'm utterly at a loss as to what to do with him. I can't blame him for being curious about the world outside and wanting to explore but I'm just so worried I might lose my job.'

'Gordon has the curiosity of a cat, but he's a good boy. He wouldn't do anything bad,' Bridie said.

'I want to nip this sort of thing in the bud, though.

Who knows where it might end! I have to work all the hours I possibly can just to make ends meet but it means I hardly get to spend any time with Gordon.'

'What can you do, Cathleen?' Bridie asked as they drank tea together by the fireplace.

'You remember Bill; the man from my past, before I came here?'

'Yes, the one with the moustache who looks like that American film star, Clark Gable?'

'He might be my only way out of here, but…' she paused before continuing: 'I haven't written to him for so many years, Bridie. I don't know how to explain myself.'

'You can only try, Cathleen. You don't know until you try.'

Mammy nodded in agreement. That night she stayed up all night writing. I didn't know who Bill was at that point, or anything about their history. I know now that my mother only ever loved two men in her life: my father, John Sullivan, and her first love, the Clark Gable lookalike, Bill Lewis.

When Bill was introduced to my mammy by her brother, Mike, all those years ago, he was smitten from the first moment. He simply couldn't take his eyes off her. It took a little while for Mammy to feel the same but she quickly came to realise how kind and lovely Bill was and they soon fell in love. Like any of us, he wasn't perfect. Bill had a keen interest in the social side of the Irish pub but he was by no means an alcoholic. Mammy didn't really like the pubs, however there was a much greater difference between them that posed a far more detrimental threat to the future of their relationship. One that had divided a nation for years. She was a Catholic and he was a Protestant. This didn't bother them, however, and they didn't let it get in the way of their love. As the months turned into years, Bill and Mammy decided they wanted to get married which meant they had to tell their families the truth. All hell broke loose with Bill's four sisters.

'We don't ever want to see or meet this woman. Don't you dare bring her into our house! What are you doing playing Romeo and Juliet? Are you out of your mind? Why can't you find a nice Protestant girl?' The reaction within Bill's home was intense.

Mammy did manage to persuade her mother to meet Bill and when she did, they got on like a house on fire. All seemed to be going well but as she was leaving the family home on the back of Bill's motorbike her mother said to her, 'Bill's a lovely man but it'll never work. He's a protestant. They're just not ready for this out there. It'd be best to look for a good Catholic man.'

Their future together was starting to appear doomed. Eventually, Bill got a job offer from London and saw this as their ticket out. He told Cathleen about the job and asked her to join him.

'What, to live in sin? My mother would never forgive me. Besides, she's old and not well. I need to be around for her.'

'I have work as a master carpenter in Pinewood Film Studios, outside of London. I'll be earning good money and can look after you. We can marry in London. Let's leave all this bigotry behind and start a new life, away from this religious madness.'

However, Cathleen couldn't bring herself to leave her sick mother whom she believed did not have long to live. She promised to keep in touch and to join Bill when he was more established in London. But as the letters became less frequent, they found themselves drifting apart and having less to write about. Then Mammy fell in love with John Sullivan, a Catholic from Cork. By the time I arrived in the world and John Sullivan had made his hasty exit, my mother had completely stopped sending letters to Bill. She was embarrassed by the whole affair and didn't want him to know about me. As the years passed, Bill continued sending letters and the odd post card to my mother every few months to her mother's address in Lucan, a village outside of Dublin.

It had been nine years since she last sent him a letter but that night, after her discussion with Bridie, Mammy found the courage to write to Bill. In her letter, she told him about me. A few weeks after that eventful night, Mammy, with the biggest smile, told me that we would be meeting her friend, Bill, at the O'Connell Bridge in the centre of Dublin next weekend. I could see a spring in her step during the week leading up to the meeting.

'Mammy, who is Bill?' I asked.

'He's an old friend I knew before you were born. He's very nice so please behave yourself when you meet him, won't you?' she replied as she combed my curly hair into place and tidied up my clothes before we left for O'Connell Bridge.

It felt like we'd been waiting for ages and still Bill did not arrive. I could see the anxious look on my mother's face.

'Let's go, Mammy, this Bill's not coming.' She kept looking at her watch.

'Wait a little longer, he will come,' she said.

I was bored and hungry. But she was right. Bill finally arrived and they behaved just like old flames. As they kissed on the famous bridge, I stood beside them in a state of shock; I had never seen Mammy kiss anybody before. It felt like a long time passed, with people beginning to stare at them.

'I'm hungry,' I shouted to catch their attention.

They broke free from their magical moment of bliss

and returned to the real world. Then Bill introduced himself.

'Let's go get something to eat then! Would you like that, Francis?'

I replied with irritation; 'My name is Gordon.' I didn't like Francis because I saw it as a girl's name. However my annoyance quickly subsided as I was pleased to be finally getting some food. Bill was definitely out to impress Mammy and me. We went to have high tea in the exclusive Shelbourne Hotel in the centre of Dublin. It was a beautiful place; I was mesmerised by the decorations and the beautiful things in the room, the likes of which I had never seen before. We had a scrumptious high tea which I still remember to this day!

'Would you like to come to see me in London for a holiday?' he asked me after some light conversation about school and such things.

'Holiday in London? I've never left Dublin. What's London like?' I asked with great excitement.'

It was all part of a bigger plan to get us out of the hostel. Mammy was hoping that Bill would accept me and invite us to join him in London. Her prayers were answered. It was a new beginning for her and a rare opportunity to give me a better life. That 'holiday' became a very long one. If I'd known we were moving to London for good and I would be leaving all my friends forever, I wouldn't have gone for sure. I often asked when we would be going back to Dublin. It was my way of dealing with the everyday struggle of living in London when things were not going well.

'When are we going back to Dublin to see all our friends again? I don't like London anymore,' I'd say.

'London is our home now, Gordon. What did I tell you before; don't talk about Regina Coeli, alright? London is the best place for you. You'll thank me for it later.'

At that time, I didn't realise how difficult it was for Mammy in Dublin. All that hiding the truth and sneaking around the city centre with me on her half-day off must have been exhausting. Looking back, we spent a lot of time watching films. It was Mammy's way of spending time with me while ensuring we didn't meet someone she might know. She made many sacrifices for me, always putting me first. I was too young to understand how lucky we were that Bill was so accepting of me. He even legally adopted me when we moved to London. Again, I didn't appreciate his sacrifice or what a hero he was, and not until later did I realise how much he loved me. I saw Bill, at first, as the man who took affection and attention from me. It took years before I warmed to him and respected him.

Even though leaving was the right thing to do, for me, Regina Coeli hostel with all its many broken windows, lack of facilities and infestation with rats, was my home. With its large open grounds and the many friends who I saw as an extended family, it was my paradise. The mothers and children made their own simple entertainment, singing Irish rebel songs about the notorious, and much feared, British Black and Tans army. We lived in absolute poverty but I didn't know anything different at the time. We, the Unfortunates, were treated with an air distain by the parents of other children from the local school. During my time living in the hostel, I never saw the inside of a house, not that I was ever invited.

Regina Coeli had a long dark history, first as a workhouse for single women and later becoming the headquarters for the Black and Tans. The barracks became derelict until Frank Duff, a radical man who believed passionately that single women should be able to keep their babies, persuaded the authorities in 1927 to allow part of the building to be used for homeless men. The building was then named Regina Coeli. In 1930 the rest of the building was used to house single mothers and their children. By 1963, the Dublin Health Authority condemned the buildings to be closed due to the many infant deaths caused by the awful conditions of the buildings. We had left for London eighteen months before.

I decided to make the best of my situation in London,

knowing I was not going back to Ireland. I soon found the streets of London to be even more exhilarating than Dublin. As an Irish boy, I spoke with a weighty Dublin accent and always called my mother, Mammy, like most Irish children. When all the other children teased me about this, I decided to give her a new name and she soon became known as Mum.

By the time I became a teenager, I had developed a new yearning to be involved with pop music.

'Gordon, can you turn your radio down please, it is far too loud.'

'But Mum, it's the Walker Brothers! "The sun ain't gonna shine anymore"...' I sang along. 'It's great Mum, don't you like it?'

'Yes, I love it, but do you have to play it so loud? The neighbours might not want to hear your brand of music, y'know. Why don't you take Brandy for his walk... and take that transistor radio with you!'

It was the hippie sixties, and young women wore very short mini-skirts and the men had long hair and flared trousers. The young talked about love, peace and sexual liberation. The new contraceptive pill gave rise to sexual freedom. The year was 1968 and Enoch Powell, the Conservative MP, had just made his controversial speech, Rivers of Blood, on immigration of Black and Asian people. This was the big news story of the year. My school friends were mostly black and born in Tottenham; an area well known for its black community as well as the famous Tottenham Hotspur Football Club. I was more of an immigrant than they were, as they were born in London, but I was white.

I was your typical working-class, suburban fifteen-year-old teenager with more than a few bad habits, still pushing my luck as far as I could. I felt much older than I was; more like twenty than fifteen. I was ready to quit school and be free of the system. I knew my future was not in academia but in seizing the opportunities out there in the big wide world. I had many wild fantasies about how I was going to make it in life.

'My God Gordon, does your mind never switch off? Please don't do anything stupid with your ideas! Did you take Brandy for his walk yet?'

The trouble was, I was still a baby-faced teenager and the only person who would take me seriously was my Mum. Well, most of the time.

Money was always tight in our home and Mum couldn't afford to give me any real pocket money because every penny went towards our rent and food. To earn money, I worked at my local newsagent on Saturdays and had paper rounds in the mornings and evenings during the week. Mum had always worked hard when we lived in Dublin and now she worked at the nearby laundry company, which didn't pay very much. I wasn't work shy, but from a young age I knew I wanted more out of life than just scraping by and I believed music would be a key part of my success.

I would hang around different record shops, looking through their selections for as long as I could, listening to what they were playing.

'Are you going to buy something today?' I was often asked.

'Yes, maybe, but I need to listen to a little bit more before I decide.'

Sometimes I would become so engrossed in the music that I would lose track of time, not realising how long I had spent in the shop until I was asked to leave. I usually got around this minor problem by going from one record shop to another, trying not to outstay my welcome. The truth was, not only did I not have the money to buy records, I didn't even own a record player! However, I could afford to buy my weekly NME newspaper with all the latest news, gossip and information about the pop stars; it had become my new bible. Music was my solace: my daydreams of a bright future and the great times that were to come. Music gave me hope.

Besides hanging out in music stores, I enjoyed going to London's famous Carnaby Street, the hip and trendy place for young people at the time. It was a bustling place, full of colourful shops selling the latest fashion. I would put on my best clothes just to go window shopping and watch the people in the street going about their business. I knew I didn't look as fashionable as those people but I vowed that one day soon I would be able to buy the clothes in these hip boutique shops, rather than just look at them!

Every evening, at the end of my newspaper round in a north London council estate, I would switch on my small transistor radio, which I carried around with me everywhere. The radio was tuned into my favourite pirate radio station, Radio Caroline, broadcasting non-stop pop music from somewhere off the coast of Britain.

My favourite DJ, Johnnie Walker, played the Radio Caroline jingle:

'C-A-R-O-L-I-N-E, Caroline, Caroline, Caroline...'

This was followed by one of my much-loved songs at the time, 'Everlasting Love' by the Love Affair group. With a great intro to the song, I got an immediate adrenaline rush. I kicked open the swing doors of the council flats to the rhythm of the classic pop record and danced my way in through the door, popping the newspapers into the letterboxes. Love Affair were my local pop group from Tottenham. It was an understatement to say I was utterly obsessed with music and wanted everybody to hear this great song on my radio.

'Time to go home and have some food! Let's see Mum.' I said to Brandy.

He would bark and jump up with excitement as if he knew exactly what I had said. Brandy would always get excited when we entered our small rented house, barking away to announce our arrival. As I entered, I could hear Bill questioning Mum about me.

'Don't you want Gordon to stay on at school? You really need to talk with him again and try to convince him to finish school and go on to university. He won't listen to me. I've tried a few times but he doesn't understand how important a degree could be for him.'

I knew Bill meant well, but I was not cut out for conventional academia and I was dyslexic, though we did not know it then. Luckily, I didn't allow this to get in my way. With my endless drive and determination, I was going to succeed no matter what.

'Bill, Gordon is single-minded and knows what he wants. Whatever I say won't change his mind,' I could hear Mum reply.

Mum knew me best. She had confidence in me and I could always rely on her to support most of my decisions.

'Hi, Mum. Hi, Bill. What's this? Talking about me leaving school again?' I greeted them with surprise as Brandy was licking their hands.

'Yes, we were talking about you and school. We want

the best for you, Gordon. Please think hard about this. You don't know how lucky you are to be able to enjoy free education until you're eighteen. I would make the most of it if I were in your position. I was just saying to Mum I think you're too young to be leaving school. What are you going to do with so little education?' I could see Bill was hoping to prompt a change of heart within me. But I knew in my heart and soul exactly what I wanted to do.

'Frankly, Bill, I don't give a damn about school! I'm leaving and that is that,' I said, quoting Clark Gable in the film, Gone with the Wind, which was one of Bill's favourite films. I didn't want to hurt Bill's feelings as I knew he only wanted the best for me, but this discussion had to stop.

Bill looked a little shocked at my assertiveness.

'Come on, Bill, you should know this boy by now. He's always fallen on his feet.' She looked at me, winked and smiled.

Mum then turned to Bill with an encouraging smile and a reassuring pat on his shoulder; 'The boy will be fine. Let's have dinner!'

Chapter Three

Free at last

I was so looking forward to my last term at school. It was going to be a repeat of the previous few years where I would turn up at school and then disappear without a trace. This was made easier by the school's system of moving students from one building to another between lessons. I saw my great escapes as a challenge to be executed with extreme precision, and although I took pride in my work, I had to keep it a secret; I never bragged about it – not even to my closest friends.

A new deputy head teacher with a reputation for being a tough enforcer arrived in my last year of school. He handed out our punishments with an old slipper on our bottoms for minor offences and with the cane for major ones. I quickly realised I had to stay off his radar or I might get found out. I lowered my profile and almost stopped the truancy altogether. It seemed to work. However, much to my dismay, the deputy head called me into his office one day.

'Damn, has he caught me out? But I was so careful, where did I go wrong?' I walked towards his room with all these questions running through my mind.

'Gordon! Take a seat,' the deputy said, without betraying any sense of emotion.

I followed his instructions promptly, with the feigned smile of a model student. My acting skills were kicking in.

'So, I hear you want to leave school at the end of this term?' I nodded in agreement before he continued. 'Would you consider changing your mind about it, Gordon?'

Gosh, he was starting to sound just like Bill. However, instead of lecturing me on the importance of education, he became somewhat of a new friend as we discussed my future. Thankfully, there was no mention of me playing truant.

'Now, Gordon, what will you do when you leave school? Let's get down to the nitty gritty. You are almost fifteen and old enough to be treated like a young adult. What kind of work are you looking to do?'

With passion in my voice, I told him I wanted to work in the music industry. But before I could tell him about my plans for getting into television, he stopped me in my tracks.

'Okay, but how are you going to get into music? What do you know about it? Can you sing or play an instrument? Can you read music?'

'No, no and no,' I replied to his last three questions.

'Come on, get that silly idea out of your head.'

He must have thought I was an idiot, fantasising about the impossible.

'You need to get yourself a real job working on the assembly lines in one of Tottenham's great factories. With your enthusiasm and hard work, you can build a good career of it. You'll appreciate my advice later in life.'

He did all the talking and I just listened, nodding and agreeing until I was able to get out of his room. I never got a moment to mention my ambition to work in television, not that I felt it would make any difference. I never stepped foot in one factory and I was back playing truant for my last few weeks of school.

I left education, as planned, at fifteen and spent the first five weeks working full time at the busy newsagent where I did my Saturday and holiday jobs. The manager wanted me to join the company as a trainee because I took more money on the tills than the rest of the staff. But I saw this as a temporary position; all I was interested in at this point was the money, which I used to buy clothes. My wonderful Italian next-door neighbour, Ollie, who I saw as one of my real teachers and mentors in my life, worked as a stagehand in the commercial television network, LWT, London Weekend Television.

'Ollie's my spy. He's looking out for a job for me as a messenger boy at the studios,' I told Mum and Bill.

Ollie had invited me to the studios in north London a few times before, when I was still at school. He was always impressed by how much I knew. I had Bill to thank for that, getting me free tickets to the theatres where he worked. During the school holidays, I would venture into different venues between productions to see and learn the workings of the theatre. I never got tired of walking around the empty theatres, looking at the photos of past and current productions lining the walls. I worked out all the kinds of jobs people did, just by watching and listening.

'Can I have a go at moving the spotlight around on stage?' I would ask the electrician. 'Can you show me how the sound works?'

I knew there was only one job I wanted to do after spending time in the theatres. I wanted to be a 'producer'; the person who could make things happen. To me, it was the most exciting and demanding job. You could be the toughest, meanest person on a set or the nicest guy in the world, depending how the production was going! I saw how producers would use charm and personality to get people to do things, whether they liked it or not.

'You definitely know how to talk and charm people, I will say that for you, Gordon. But you need to get a real job,' Bill said when I told him what job I would like most. 'You don't just become a producer. You need the qualifications and experience,' he added. I believe Bill thought I was dreaming way out of my league and he was unsure how I was going to make it happen.

On the sixth week after leaving school, Ollie alerted me to a vacancy for a messenger boy at LWT studios. My luck was in. Bill insisted he would take a day off work to go with me to the interview. This meant he would lose a day's money, which we needed.

'What will people think of me, bringing you along for my big interview? Please don't come, Bill.' I was begging him.

This time, Mum was on Bill's side and at the very last moment, I reluctantly agreed to let Bill join me. We turned up at the studios, which had a wealth of history. My favourite pop music show, RSG, Ready Steady Go! went out live every Friday evening here with music from Dave Clark Five, The Who, The Animals, and artists from the USA like The Supremes and Otis Reading. I watched this programme without fail.

Bill sat next to me in the LWT reception area reading his favourite tabloid paper, the Mirror, as I looked around pretending I didn't know him. After almost half an hour of waiting an older man from the administration, who was dressed in a smart three-piece suit, invited me into a small side room with an air of authority. Bill looked at me, smiling and let the cat out of bag; 'Good luck, Gordon.'

'Is that your father?'

'No, I don't know him, he was just chatting to me.'

The man sat down at a desk and said in an extremely posh English accent, 'Sorry old boy, bad news. We've had, what we call in television, a mix up. We conducted the interviews yesterday and have already chosen a young man for the job. Come back next time when there's another opening.'

I felt as if the wind had been knocked out of me. This was not in the script! Utterly at a loss for words, I sat there clutching my interview letter desperately trying to think of what to say.

'Are you not going to interview me today?' I asked finally. Perhaps I could change his mind.

'I'm afraid not, old boy,' he answered without much sympathy and with a touch of condescension. He seemed to find my question amusing. It was definitely not funny and I hated the way he kept saying 'old boy'. I wanted to tell him, 'You're the old boy, not me!'

I was angry but I didn't want to show my true feelings. Without saying another word, he escorted me out of the room telling me he had a very busy day ahead of him. When I arrived back in the reception, alone, Bill looked up from reading his newspaper; 'That didn't take long. How did it go?'

I couldn't look at him. 'Can we talk about this outside? Stop asking questions and let's get out of here!'

My despondent face gave the game away. My confidence and unyielding self-belief had been shattered for the first time. I was incensed and wanted to swear but I knew Bill wouldn't like that. No conversation ensued until halfway through the Underground train journey home.

'It is not the end of the world, Gordon. There will be other jobs and interviews. You're just starting out and you're still very young.'

I knew Bill was right but it really did feel like my dream had been crushed before it even got going. I remained silent, looking out of the window. If Bill hadn't been on the train with me, I think I would have cried. This was a real learning experience for me; my first major rejection in life. Up until now, I had always got what I set out to get.

When we got home, Bill went off to the pub. He was

perhaps in need of a drink after trying unsuccessfully to console me. I took Brandy for a long walk with my radio to see Mum at the shop. As I got nearer, Johnnie Walker played Dusty Springfield's big hit, 'I Close My Eyes and Count to Ten'. To me she was the sixties, with her famous beehive hairstyle and dark heavy eye makeup. I walked into the laundry shop and I turned off my radio; Johnnie had caught my mood with his last song. Mum knew immediately something was wrong. She was wearing her white uniform and had a new hairstyle, like Dusty's. Over a cup of tea, she put everything into perspective; being positive was her real talent. On the bus home she said, 'Gordon, I have two things to say. See this as a dry run for the next interview at the studios. Believe me, you'll have more rejections to come in life. You just have to persevere and make your luck happen. You can't give up easily if you're to get anywhere in life.' She was very persuasive.

Working full-time at the newsagent was better than being in school but Bill did not see this as a real job. I felt guilty that I wasn't earning more money to contribute to living at home. The shop manager had promised me a pay rise until the head office decided to freeze all increments. For the first time since I left school, I felt my world was falling apart.

After my horribly disappointing week with no

interview and no pay rise, I went to the Irish Catholic Social Club in north London with my close friends Brian and Gerard Greene to have an inexpensive night out. It was a Saturday evening and we were all broke teenagers, but we knew we could always get free drinks from the paddies. Gerard, the older of the two brothers, was my best friend and more of a drinker. Brian was always happy to go with the flow. When I first arrived in London from Dublin, they were my next-door neighbours and their caring parents, Kate and Mick, always treated me like an extension to their family. Mick arrived with the first free drinks.

The smoky club was packed and there was only one subject on everybody's lips: Northern Ireland and the civil rights action by the Catholics, which became known as 'The Troubles', with the Protestants and Catholics fighting each other. Occurring at the same time in America were the race riots about civil rights. There was speculation about the Irish Republican Army (IRA) using some form of guerrilla warfare on the streets of Britain. It was not a great time to be Irish and there was a nervousness in the air about what might happen next.

The live music started up with a local band and one of the older Irishmen got up on stage and started singing a well-known Irish song, 'Whiskey in the Jar' to change the mood of the evening. The crowd joined in as I looked around the room, watching all the tough Irish labourers buying drinks like there was no tomorrow.

'Brian, Gerard, Gordon, what are you drinking?' asked one of the men at the bar seeing our empty glasses. Brian gave me a wink, meaning we were on for more free drinks.

'Thanks, pints all round please,' said Brian, and this was just the start of the evening.

All the men were dressed in smart shirts and suits for their big night out. You wouldn't think most of them worked on London building sites or dug up roads as labourers. They did the dirty hard work nobody wanted to do; their reward was cash payments with no tax to pay. There were two types of Irish men: the young single ones who were into heavy drinking and partying and the ones who would save their money to go back to Ireland and build homes for themselves or start new families. In the late sixties, you couldn't walk around London without hearing Irish voices or seeing them digging up the roads and building the new underground train lines.

I noticed Martin Flatley, a very likeable Irishman whose job was to hire and fire men for one of the many Irish construction companies. He was an important man in the Irish community and men would look to him for work. He was also related to the Greenes. Martin was the only Irishman I knew who did not drink alcohol but could still dish out delightfully funny Irish stories and jokes.

'Hello, Gordon. What are you up to?' he asked as I approached him.

'I've left school and I'm hoping to get into the television industry one day. But I need a job from you to tide me over,' I said, matter-of-factly.

Martin thought I was drunk. He was amused and made fun of me, 'You're only a boy! You won't last one day with the heavy digging,' he said, still laughing at me.

'Come on, Martin, you must have something I can do. I really need a job.' I used all my charm on him.

'There's a vacancy for a tea boy. No heavy digging involved but—' I immediately accepted the offer before he could even begin telling me the downsides.

'Can you cook? And how old are you now?' Martin still had doubt in his voice as he looked down at me.

'I'm sixteen. And of course I can cook, I help Mum with the cooking all the time. She's always working long hours, you see!'

I continued my cheekiness and asked Martin for the same rate as the paddies, which he was generous enough to agree to. I was making my luck happen, just like Mum had told me. For the rest of the evening, my mind was on all the new clothes I would be able buy in London's Carnaby Street. I always thought I knew how to make situations work to my advantage, but I really didn't know what I was getting myself into.

Chapter Four
Paddies

I arrived home in the early hours of Sunday morning to find Brandy had taken the liberty of making himself at home on my bed. He was obviously too comfortable to get up and greet me, instead thumping his great tail on the bed excitedly. As I tried to sandwich myself between the sheets, he began licking my hands and wagging his tail even more. 'Brandy, stop! Leave me alone,' I whispered, tying not to wake anyone. Eventually, we both manage to squeeze into my bed, though it was a bit of a struggle because Brandy was not a small dog! It was like sharing a bed with a giant, panting teddy bear.

The next morning, over a full Irish breakfast, Mum enquired why I had been so late coming home. She didn't miss a trick. It was as if she had eyes in the back of her head.

'I was schmoosing about the Social Club and I've found myself a great paying job. I start Monday morning, early,' I said smugly.

Mum's reaction was immediately positive, as was Bill's. However, the mood quickly changed when I mentioned I would be working as a teaboy on a construction site, cooking for the men.

'Oh, Gordon, you're not going to work with the navvies, are you?' Bill remarked in total dismay and stopped eating his breakfast in favour of a cigarette.

Mum was similarly surprised but continued to ask about the job.

'How in the name of Jesus, Mary and Joseph did you get Martin Flatley to pay you the same rate as the navvies? Maybe working with the paddies will do you some good, and the money does sound fantastic,' she said with amusement and a kiss on my head.

Bill was not impressed, certain that this job would be entirely unfitting. He had always wanted more for me than this sort of work, which is why he pushed me to stay in school.

'Now Bill Lewis, don't be such an Irish snob. Gordon's found a job and he'll learn a lot from the experience; it's not permanent anyway,' she remarked.

Both Mum and I could only snigger as Bill brusquely got up and left the table. He was sulking and left to take

Brandy out for his Sunday morning walk without saying another word.

'You're not exactly a cook, are you Gordon? How will you feed those men?' she asked in her gentle way after the door closed behind Bill. She did have a point.

On Monday morning, I set my alarm clock for an early start. The government authorities had closed down the pirate radio station and my favourite DJ, Johnnie Walker had gone missing. Instead I could only listen to BBC Radio, which played very little pop music. I woke up at 5am listening to 'Good Morning, Good Morning', a song from the Gene Kelly movie, Singing in the Rain. It was played every morning at the same time. I decided to put on my second-best clothes for work. I walked up to the top of my road as the sun rose over the small terraced houses and waited for Martin to collect me in his car.

'Good morning, Gordon, are you ready for work? Don't let me down.'

Before I could say anything, he started singing along to Irish music on his car cassette player. We arrived in Camden Town, one of the many meeting points for Irish workers from all over the north London area.

I had no real idea what I was letting myself in for. It was a massive culture shock seeing hundreds of Irish men waiting to be told which white Ford van or big open trucks they would be travelling to work in. It was like one big open-air employment exchange with paymasters like Martin, known as the Ganger men, who were responsible for hiring men. It was a lively and rowdy atmosphere.

'Pretend you don't know me but keep close to me, and don't lend anybody money. Remember what I'm saying,' Martin said.

The scene was a little overwhelming with men constantly coming up to Martin asking for work. He gave them the same reply each time: 'Get in line. I told you before, if you want work, get in line.' He was tough and handled all of the men's questions and complaints in roughly the same manner.

'You've had your chance, no.' He knew each and every man's drinking and fighting habits.

'How about a sub, boss?' meaning a loan. Back came a firm 'no' from Martin.

Men of different ages were standing against the shop windows waiting for their names to be called. Martin, in his smart dark suit with a pen and notebook in hand, started to point to the men and called out their names in a military manner.

'Murphy, O'Connell, Doherty, Sullivan, Donoghue, Boyle and Kelly.'

Martin introduced me to my supervisor – a man from Wexford named John, who was in charge of twenty-five or more men.

'John, this is your new teaboy, Gordon. Keep an eye on him, he could charm his way into Heaven without going to church.'

I quickly jumped into the front seat of the white Ford van with ten big paddies in the back. I felt overdressed and out of place as the men stared at me. We left in a convoy in two big trucks with the workers standing up and holding on to whatever they could. The men would talk in English and Gaelic, the Irish language, about what they had done over the weekend.

'I bet you're a Liverpool fan,' one of them said. Before I could reply, another voice interrupted, 'No, he must be a Manchester United fan.' All the paddies adored Liverpool and Manchester football clubs. Somebody said, 'He must be an Arsenal fan if he is Irish.'

I was a part Tottenham and part Arsenal fan; having lived in the two areas, my loyalty was divided. Banter played a big part in the morning drive to work.

We arrived in Uxbridge, on the edge of London, and I found myself standing in the middle of some green fields. There was to be no tea or coffee before work began. Within minutes, John had organised the men to start laying cables and pipes. The heavy digging was done with shovels and picks.

'We're going shopping for food, Teaboy, get in the van.' John was a man of few words. I don't think he liked me!

'I understand you can cook. Where did you cook last?'

'Erm, at home,' I stammered. John didn't look impressed.

'Well, you're on your own tomorrow, Teaboy.' He never called me by my actual name.

We arrived in Uxbridge town and bought beef steaks for breakfast, and lamb chops and sausages for lunch. Large packs of tea, sugar and loaves of white bread. When we got back to the construction site I looked around for the kitchen and the toilet.

'John, where will I find the toilet?' He found my question very funny and pointed to two small wooden box-like cabins at the end of another field. One was the toilet and the other, the kitchen.

When I saw the so-called toilet, which consisted of a dirty metal bucket on the floor with no lock on the door, I could see why he had laughed at my question. Both small cabins were without any windows. My 'kitchen' had a large gas bottle connected to a gas ring sitting on the dirty wooden floor. A clean metal bucket and a huge frying pan sat next to piles of white enamel cups and plates. The enamelware reminded me of my days growing up in the hostel in Dublin.

'Alright Teaboy, I'm no cook. I will only show you once how everything works, do you understand me?'

As John was about to start cooking, I looked for a broom or something to clean the dirty floor.

'Teaboy, don't worry about the floor! Just get the fucking tea ready, they'll want the tea first,' he shouted.

He emptied a full packet of tea bags into the metal bucket of boiling water, followed by a full bottle of milk.

'This is how the paddies like their tea, with lots of sugar.' he said, adding a full packet of sugar to the tea and stirring it around with a large bread knife.

John bent down to put the steaks onto the hot pan. He was a cumbersome man and started to complain about his back pains when he dropped a couple of steaks onto the floor. All I could do was look on in amazement, rooted to the spot, as he picked them up out of the dirt and put them back in the pan.

'A little bit of dirt won't hurt the fucking paddies,' said John, after catching the look on my face. 'They just want to eat and they'll eat anything you give 'em, as long as it's fucking meat.'

It didn't take me long to realise that John used the foulest words imaginable when he was stressed. For these men, this sort of language was simply routine. My first morning on the job was not as bad as I had anticipated. The men didn't say much; their minds were on tea and food. The breakfast was polished off very quickly and then the men began asking for more tea and bread.

Some even wanted more steaks.

'For fuck's sake, you just ate two big steaks. You want more?' John said in his usual rough manner.

John told me he needed to go to the bank. I asked him to pick up some cleaning material, a broom, and a few other things. He just laughed.

'You're going to make a nice profit at the end of each week from selling the food you cook, on top of your wages. I'll give you a sub to start, pay me back at the end of the week.'

By the end of my first week, I was proud to have my first salary. I was also working out my profit on the food sales but I seemed to be coming up a bit short.

'Ten of the men haven't paid me for the week and they aren't with us anymore,' I informed John, hoping he might help.

'That's your fucking problem. I'm not your bank manager. Next time get the money up front, Teaboy! If not, you'll lose money.'

I did make a profit that week, and started paying more attention to the cost of what I was buying and the money I was collecting. The great part of my job was that I could leave after lunch, taking the Underground back to London. The worst part of the job was having to empty out the other bucket in the second cabin, the toilet. I would dump the contents onto the green field, away from where the men were working. I almost threw up the first few times but eventually I got used to it, although I could never bring myself to actually use the toilet.

By Tuesday or Wednesday, many of the men would ask me for a sub. Being bachelors, drinking and gambling were very much part of their lives and they liked to keep money reserved for such activities.

'Teaboy, can I pay you for breakfast and lunch at the end of the week?'

'No, you get a sub from John, don't ask me again.'

'But Teaboy, I need the money for tonight.' That meant drinks.

'Well, no food for you then. Don't touch my food!' I would snap.

Overnight I became a lot tougher and John would look on with great amusement, watching my progress. Martin arrived for breakfast one morning and John told him how well I was doing. Martin congratulated me and asked for his breakfast, and I put out my hand for payment.

'What?! I'm your paymaster, Gordon,' he exclaimed.

'John always pays for his meals, isn't that right, John?'

Martin was speechless but he could see the funny side.

'You taught him far too well, John.' From that day, I must have earned John's respect because he started calling me Gordon.

I found banter was always the key when dealing with the men. That was until one day when a big paddy wasn't interested in my policy of paying up front. His nickname was Monster because he was bigger and taller than the average man. When my back was turned, he helped himself to two steaks from my frying pan and almost knocked me over. The men knew I did not allow anybody into the cabin or to touch the food. These were my rules.

'Don't fuck with my kitchen or my food!' I shouted.

'Go tell him, Teaboy.' The men laughed.

Monster was about to sit down to eat my juicy steaks when I snatched the plate of food away from him. The gigantic man was incandescent with rage. He towered above me, glaring down with fury. As his boulder-sized fist went up in the air, John shouted out, 'Don't you fuck with the teaboy or you'll have twenty men on you; they all want their fucking lunch later. Just fucking pay the teaboy for the food, Monster!' I was lucky not to get a fist in my face that morning. Monster finally paid up and all the other men fell about crying with laughter until they had stiches at the sight of him eating humble pie.

After a few weeks, the men were asking for something different to eat. So I cooked bacon, eggs and black pudding as a trial. They thought they were in paradise. After successfully testing the market, the following week

I started charging for the 'extras'.

'No more freebies, you want extras, you pay for them.' They all paid and my profits went up.

Going home on the train, I started to notice people would move away from me. I realised I looked like a tramp and had begun to resemble an older version of one of the 'unfortunate' Irish children I had grown up with in Regina Coeli. Mum was getting worried about my unkempt looks, uncouth language and the behaviour which I seem to have acquired from the job. Bill had almost given up on me. He was afraid I would continue working with the paddies because of the lure of good money. However, the cold winter days were starting to bite; I needed to find a job indoors.

There was no sign of a television job coming my way but, within a week of leaving the paddies, I landed a job behind the counter of an old-fashioned delicatessen shop. The white overcoat uniform was far too big for me and I desperately wanted to cut off the rolled-up sleeves, which always got in my way. When teenagers came into the shop they would look at me and whisper among themselves, which made me feel silly and self-conscious.

The manager thought I knew how to sell the meats and cheeses, but oh, how I hated the smell of the cheese! He wanted me to become a trainee manager, which was all very flattering, but I was already losing interest in retail. The indecisive female customers constantly changing their minds: 'Make it a bigger piece, no, I've changed my mind, give me that smaller one. No, I'll take the first one!' The men were always easier to serve. I quickly realised women did things differently, and if I wanted my bonus, I had to give the women much more attention. But even with the bonus, I'd soon had enough of the smelly cheeses and the terrible money so I left the job after four weeks. I had conjured up another plan in my mind to make real money, and fast.

'Mum, I have this great idea for a business. It's to do with music; you know how much I love music. You and Bill won't ever need to work again, I'm going to make loads of money!' I gabbled at my default setting of 100mph.

Bill just rolled his eyes and carried on reading his paper while I continued talking about this new business venture. Mum paid more attention to my spiel while trying to hide her concern and doubt so that she didn't upset me. It was only two years previously, at the age of fourteen, that I had wanted to join one of the many pirate radio stations based out at sea and become a DJ like my hero, Johnnie Walker.

My new idea had come from attending the Catholic Church club nights on Saturday evenings, near Arsenal's football ground in north London. Although I had stopped attending church, I still liked going to the church hall and dancing to the music. However the records they played were always old and the music was never loud enough for us teenagers. The parents and priests were always around to ensure the boys were kept at a safe distance from the girls, which undoubtedly put a limit on the sort fun you could have. The boys would turn the lights down to make it more atmospheric only for a priest or a parent to turn them up again. There was no alcohol; only soft drinks were served.

Having gained more confidence from working with the paddies, my idea was to start my own nightclub. I was going to spice things up, allowing the teenagers to do all the things they couldn't do at the church club. There would be alcohol, dim lighting, the boys and girls could get close, and the music would be deafeningly loud.

I was quite certain my plan would work so, after deciding to put it into motion with immediate effect, I went searching for a suitable venue. I must have gone to about ten different pubs in north London, all on my own, and unsurprisingly none were interested in my proposal. I had just turned sixteen but still I maintained that pesky baby face. The landlords were all taken aback by my request.

'You what? You want my venue for a teenage nightclub? You must be joking! How old are you? You don't look old enough to wear trousers, let alone run a nightclub.'

None of the abusive comments put me off. I knew I looked too young to be taken seriously so I decided to invite my Greek Cypriot friend, George, to tag along when I approached the pub owners because he was much taller and looked older than me.

George would get paid if we made money, but he was just happy for the opportunity to meet the girls.

After a few weeks of approaching numerous pubs, I found what I was looking for.

'I'm very proud of my upstairs bar, Gordon. It's my favourite part of the pub,' Gloria, the managers wife, said. She was especially proud of the lovely red curtains draping the large windows on the second floor. I used all my magic to persuade Gloria that I would deliver enough young people to spend heaps of money at her venue every Saturday night. The pub would make money from the sales of alcohol and I would keep all the entrance money. That was my deal, and she agreed.

'Don't forget, only invite nice young people, okay?' she said as I looked around the lounge.

'It's perfect, Gloria, and you're right, it's beautiful,' I said, as though I was her best friend. It was the only pub that agreed to let me run my nightclub.

I networked day and night for several weeks before the first Saturday club night, visiting other Catholic churches and talking to school fiends, inviting anyone to attend. I kept telling the boys, 'lots of birds will be there, lads!' And as for the girls, I was offering free entrance for the opening night.

I was really nervous as I walked to the venue the night we were due to open. I was more worried about making a fool of myself at this point, rather than making money, as my pride was at stake. However, I had one big smile on my face when I saw the long queue forming outside the pub before the doors opened.

The venue looked really classy with the dim lighting and the music sounded great; it was certainly loud. The deep red curtains were drawn, it felt like an intimate and private place for teenagers to have fun, away from the peering eyes of parents and adults! The DJ was a friend of mine who shared the same tastes in music as me. He played mostly imported American soul records, Motown, and R&B. My black school friends who attended were influenced by Jamaican Reggae music of the star icons like Jimmy Cliff and Desmond Dekker. I dressed like a white soul boy that night with my skinhead haircut, which was all the craze with the alternative crowd. My mohair trousers and Ben Sherman shirts were all part of my new look; the cool club owner. The club night was called Eureka.

I had decent takings at the door that night and the

landlady was impressed with the drink sales behind the bar. Two weeks into the arrangement, Gloria tried to change the deal.

'You have to pay for the hire of my upstairs lounge bar; you must be making a mint with all those teenagers paying to get in.'

'No way, Gloria, I'll find a new venue. Other people will be queueing up to offer me a place to run this club night,' I told her firmly but politely. She relented and kept to the original deal.

I was soon back in swinging Carnaby Street buying more clothes, shirts, and trousers. I could even afford to buy the new Brut 33 fragrance in a plastic bottle, as advertised on television by the famous British boxer Henry Cooper. Every teenager wanted to be my new best friend, hoping to get in for free. But as I had learnt from my experience working with the paddies, nobody got in without paying.

On the fifth Saturday, George was confronted by two older guys refusing to pay at the door.

'They're not the kind you would want to pick a fight with, Gordon. I had to let them in. I told them to enjoy themselves and not cause trouble, and they said they wouldn't,' said a panicky George.

Within less than ten minutes, the two young men were throwing their weight around and demanding free drinks.

'Hey mate, how's it going? Do you like my new club?' I asked, knowing I had to deal with the situation.

'What! This is your club?' They started laughing.

'Just f-off little boy, we're taking over your club. Get lost!'

I was completely flabbergasted. Without wanting to aggravate the situation further and risk being pulverised by these idiots, I made my way over to three older and bigger guys I knew from Tottenham, one of whom was the local champion boxer.

'Hi, Steve, enjoying the night? Would you and your mates like to earn some easy money tonight? I'll even throw in some free drinks and introduce you to some girls.'

They were all keen on the offer. I pointed to the two guys at the bar; 'I want you to remove those two troublemakers. Try not to start a fight though, wouldn't be good for my business, you know. Just let them know you want them off the premises.'

Steve and his mates walked over to the two guys and within minutes, they were out. I was very impressed with how Steve and his friends handled the situation without escalating things.

The nightclub was going from strength to strength; the queues would stretch around the corner of the building with everybody paying to get in. The crowd was changing from people I knew to strangers who had come from different schools and areas further afield. I started to hear talk of 'speed', the drug that teenagers at that time were getting into. Drugs were all new to me, but I was never tempted to try them.

A couple of weeks later, the two troublemakers returned, but this time they paid to get in.

'The two guys who caused trouble a while back are here with some other friends of theirs, but they all paid to get in. That's a good sign, right?' George came running to me after their arrival.

'Damn, George, I don't like the look of their friends, they look like a gang. I think they're here to cause more problems! You leave now and take the money box with you, before they come looking for me. I have a nasty feeling something bad is going to happen.'

Sure enough, a fight broke out ten minutes later. The first piece of furniture thrown across the room smashed the large gold-framed mirror that hung over the bar. Screams and shouts followed, with everyone rushing for the door. The gang of youths went for the bottles of alcohol behind the bar and grabbed as many as they could. Hearing screams and loud crashing, Gloria came running up the stairs pushing her way into the crowd only to see them smashing and looting her lovely bar.

'No! No! Not my curtains!' she screamed at the top of her voice when the thugs pulled her beloved red drapes to the ground.

Hiding around the corner, watching the scene unfold, I couldn't believe what was happening. I felt sorry for Gloria as she wept on the floor holding onto her curtains. She was powerless as she watched the gang destroying the place and looting her bar.

I ran for the fire exit as fast as I could to meet George who was waiting for me nearby with the money box. We ended up in the Wimpy bar near my home to enjoy a late-night burger to calm our nerves. All good things come to an end and it certainly looked like this was the end of my career as a club promoter. Nobody would ever trust me with their venue now!

Chapter Five

Basement to the stars

Christmas was fast approaching, and I was contemplating having my first holiday with the money I earned from the paddies and the nightclub venture. I told Mum I wanted to go to Ireland to spend some time with her sister, Lilly, omitting to tell her the real reason for my visit.

When we came to live in London, Mum made it clear to me she never wanted to talk about our earlier life in Dublin. I guess there were too many sad memories from her past and she was desperately trying to move on. When we first moved to London, I would often try to talk about Dublin as I missed the friends I had left behind. But a quick flash from my Mum's bright blue eyes would silence me in an instant; 'Now, what did I tell you before, Gordon. No more talk about Regina Coeli!

Just look ahead of you, to the future.'

I did stop asking about the past but my strong romantic feelings for Ireland and the people there never left me. This short holiday was for me to try and find my former home and my best friends, Joe and Conner: my two amigos. We had made a special pact; 'Friends for life', we'd said. I was hoping I would find them as I hadn't seen them since we left Dublin, seven years ago.

So, I spent Christmas of 1968 with my mother's sister, Lilly. I had forgotten how slow and sleepy Ireland was compared to London. Aunt Lilly lived in a small town called Maynooth to the west of Dublin. It was famous for St Patrick's College, which trained hundreds of Catholic priests every year. Within days of my arrival, I made my way into Dublin by bus. As I watched the world go by through the window, I wondered what my friends might look like now. Joe was older than me and had always wanted to become a priest. I later found out he had moved on from this idea after the death of his mother, becoming a trainee jeweller instead. As for Conner, it was quite possible that he would be in jail for fighting or some such thing. He was always a bit of a hothead. Unfortunately I never did find out what became of him.

I had thought it would be easy to find the hostel in the north part of Dublin, but I couldn't have been more wrong. Walking up and down the streets, I searched for something familiar. I jumped on and off of various buses trying to find the place I had grown up in. But my efforts were fruitless and I left Dublin that evening, disappointed.

Two days later I told Aunt Lilly I was going to Dublin again to buy her a lovely present, and off I went again. I spent several hours searching for the hostel until I had the idea of asking the nuns and priests gathered in the busy city centre.

'Hello, can you help me please? I'm looking for a hostel for single mothers on the north side of old Dublin. Do you know it?' I asked them, politely.

The absolute shock and horror on their faces said it all. They quickly walked away from me like I was a bad smell. I had forgotten what it was like to live here under the grip of the Catholic Church, with its pervading influence on the Irish people. I decided that I was perhaps destined never to meet my two friends again. From that day on, I finally turned the page on Regina Coeli and that part of my life, closing the chapter without a substantial feeling of closure.

The next weekend I decided to visit Bill's mother and his only unmarried sister, Jenny, who lived together on the south side of Dublin in Donnybrook. Bill had asked me to go and visit them. He now overlooked the way his sisters had treated his relationship with Mum. 'Life is far too short to keep agonising about your sisters. You need to move on, Bill,' Mum always said to him. She had helped him repair the relationship with his four sisters in spite of their prejudice against her. They were now talking to each other again after many years of silence.

Over tea and cakes with Auntie Jenny and her mother, I was given a warm Irish welcome. However, she was curious to know more about my past and would bombard me with her typically intrusive Irish questioning. But Mum had taught me well and I could easily slip into acting mode to evade even her most direct attacks.

'Do you not remember when you were here last? Where in Ireland did you grow up, or was it in England?' Jenny asked as I stuffed myself with more of her lovely homemade cakes.

The questions were not new to me; I always pretended I couldn't remember my past to avoid giving any real answers. I grew up without knowing my father, like all the children in the hostel. The only men we would see at the hostel were the new priests in the area coming to see how we lived. There were also the dustbin men who would come to collect the rubbish. We would cheekily ask them, while sitting on the steps outside the big wooden doors of the hostel, 'Hello Mister, are you my daddy?'

Most of the men would just smile back and get on with their work, but others would curse at us and call us 'little bastards'. We all hated this word and would curse back at anyone who said it.

'Are you going to see your Aunt Susie? I'm sure she would like to see you,' Jenny asked. Bill had very little time for Susie; their relationship was still fraught. In the past he had called her evil because of the offensive things she said to him about Mum.

I decided to make my way to visit Susie in Blackrock, a very nice well-to-do area on the outskirts of Dublin with attractive houses and manicured lawns. I pushed the doorbell and a small, trim, bespectacled woman with deep lines on her face came to the door.

For almost fifteen minutes, she spoke to me at the door. I could see her lounge leading onto her pretty garden. However, there was no friendly Irish welcome like at Jenny's or Lilly's. Susie was cold as ice. 'I need to go, or I'll be late for the church,' she said, when she finally ran out of things to say. And with that, she closed her front door on me.

After the New Year celebrations over at Lilly's, which was a very boozy Irish affair, I returned home to London, feeling a little down without the prospect of a job in the television or music industry in sight. It was 1969, the year when the first man stepped on the moon, and I knew I would need to put Plan B into operation as my money was running out.

I looked through the newspapers for a job and to my

delight, I saw a vacancy for a trainee photographer. I thought it could be interesting and somewhat in keeping with television. When I was working as the teaboy, I went to photography night classes with my friend Brian, so I had some knowledge of the field. Bill was ecstatic when I told him about the interview for the photography job.

'At last, a real job as a professional trainee, good on you! Hope you get the job.'

I knew he was pleased I had taken his advice and not gone back to work with the paddies, despite the great money.

'Bill, my dream is still to work in television and music, but for now I'll make the best of my situation,' I said.

'Sometimes it is all about whether your face fits, and discrimination happens in everyday life; don't forget that and rise above it.' Bill was talking about how Irish people were often treated when looking for work and somewhere to live in London. 'Gordon, forget about big money this time, start at the bottom, you'll learn on the job and not look back. You're making the right decision,' he assured me.

I made my way into the centre of London for my interview with the boss of the company, a Mr A.K. Ware. I was a little concerned that there was no mention of salary in the advertisement. Mr Ware was on the phone when I arrived so the secretary stopped typing and asked me some questions while I waited.

'What do your father and mother do?'

I replied with pride and a big grin on my face; 'My father works in the theatre as a master carpenter and Mum is a shop supervisor for Western in north London.'

Her eyes lit up and she nodded as if to show she was very impressed. However, when she realised I was talking about Western the laundry company, and not the chemist, she seemed less impressed. She stopped talking to me and continued typing. I knew she was a snob.

When I finally went into Mr Ware's office, I couldn't believe how enormous he was; like a baby elephant. He shook my hand and asked me to sit down. His phone kept ringing during the interview and each time he had difficulty reaching it. I was tempted to help him pick it up but I decided I'd better not! I could tell he was impressed with my knowledge of the theatre and my night classes in photography. Strategically, I decided to omit the time I spent as a teaboy with the paddies. Within less than twenty minutes, Mr Ware told me I had the job.

'Looking forward to seeing you here bright and early next Monday,' he said.

'What about the salary, Mr Ware?' I enquired.

'I am investing in you, Gordon. As a trainee, you will learn all the necessary skills to become a professional photographer. You'll have a wonderful future working for my company.' I remained in my chair, weighing up the situation.

'But Mr Ware, I cannot work without any salary,' I protested.

'You will be paid expenses for your travel and lunch, and there is a token amount towards your upkeep. Remember, like all the young men here, you are starting at the bottom and learning to work your way up.'

I was shocked by the money; the sum was much less than my delicatessen job, which was bad enough. I was having second thoughts about taking the job but Bill's words were ringing in my ears.

'Thank you, Mr Ware. See you Monday.' I walked out of the large office and headed home, not overly pleased.

I wasn't sure if I should be celebrating the new job, what with the disappointing pay, but Mum and Bill were both extremely pleased and I was glad to have made them happy – especially Bill.

On my first day, all dressed in my Sunday best, I found myself stuck in the basement with no windows or natural light. I was on my feet, drying out black and white photos on a large machine until lunchtime. Before I went to eat, I was expected to fetch Mr Ware's lunch from the restaurant next door and deliver it to him on a tray at his desk. He had food enough for two! For the rest of the day, I was stuck doing the same task in the dark basement.

At the end of the first week I received my salary of six pounds, after tax. I had been earning five pounds every day, in cash, working with the paddies on the construction site, and that was before the extra money from the food sales. Looking at the six pounds, I decided to ask the secretary if I could see Mr Ware.

'What's the matter, Gordon, why do you need to see Mr Ware?'

'Personal matter,' I said, standing my ground.

When he had finished on the phone, I made my point about the cost of travel.

'With only six pounds a week, Mr Ware, I have no spare money to live on. I have a retired elderly father and mother who need contributions from me towards the home,' I exaggerated the situation and put on a very sad face. Indeed, I read this man like a book.

'Okay, I'll give you food vouchers to help you get by. Now run along and get back to your work!'

In my second week, I made friends with some of the older employees who had worked there for a few years. I was sounding them out to see when I might be able to do some actual photography.

'It could take years before you get to work with the camera! The boss likes to keep his boys drying photographs and hand delivering them to the clients for as long as he can,' one of them told me.

I was not going to wait years; I saw this as cheap labour for the company. Having received my second week's wages, I decided it was time to see the boss again. His protector, the secretary, peered at me over the top of her glasses.

'Not you again. What is it this time?'

'Personal matter,' I replied again, with a straight face. I remained planted to the spot until she let me see him.

'Mr Ware, I'm still finding it impossible to get by on what I'm being paid, even with the food vouchers. But I'm hungry to learn. I've been doing the same job in the basement for the last two weeks.'

'Look,' he interjected, 'you can't expect to progress that fast; there's so much to learn in the basement before you start anything with the camera.'

'I've learnt everything there is to do in the basement, Mr Ware. I learn quickly and get bored very easily,' I continued, undeterred.

Mr Ware looked at me for quite some time, leaning back in his chair. 'I've never come across a trainee like you.'

I maintained his gaze with just the right amount of pitifulness and defiance as he scorned me for my audacity. Eventually he yielded.

'Alright, I'll give you another pound towards your salary, but I don't want to see you in here again for some time!' he added after calming down a little.

As the weeks crawled by, my job began to feel more and more like a prison sentence. I was really jaded by the relentless, mind-numbing routine of drying black and white photos in the horrible basement. One day I spoke to another senior staff member who was honest and helpful.

'I don't blame you for feeling frustrated. I only got to touch a camera after two years of doing what you're doing now.'

On Thursday evening, I told Mum and Bill I was going to ask for another salary increase. Bill was dumbfounded.

'You have some front, Gordon, how could you ask again? Three times in three weeks! You can't be serious.' He sounded just like the boss, telling me off for my cheekiness!

'How did Mr Ware react,' Mum asked, ignoring Bill's outburst.

'Let's put it this way; he wasn't particularly happy and he lost his cool with me. But he did give me an extra pound,' I said.

Bill was in a state of fury, shaking his head in disbelief. I knew I was pushing my luck in more ways than one but it had reached the point where I actually wanted to be sacked. At five minute intervals I was looking at the large clock on the wall of the basement, wishing the hours to pass quickly so I could escape sooner. I felt like an ensnared animal. The job was killing me; it was almost worse than school, the only difference was I could always skip school.

Just as I was feeling at my lowest, my prayers were finally answered. Ollie came around to our house one Sunday evening to inform me about an opening for a messenger boy at the studios.

'The last messenger boy lost his job because he refused to cut his long hair. Youngsters of today, huh? Well, Gordon, your short haircut will go down well with the head of the post room, that's for sure. You just have to convince the interviewers you're the right person for the job,' Ollie assured me.

The next morning, I made a telephone call from the local public telephone box to the personnel department at LWT. I wanted to make sure I was on the list of interviewees for the job, citing the fact I wasn't given the opportunity to be interviewed last time. I was ecstatic; my interview was organised for the Thursday and I could not wait.

Because of the telephone call, I was late to work. The secretary stared at me derisively as I arrived but I didn't care. I just told her I was delayed because of the bus and went straight down into the prison basement to do my work.

Thursday soon came around and Mum gave me some of her infallible advice; 'Remember, timing is everything in life. Make that luck work for you.'

I arrived early at the studios for the noon interview. Bill was not with me this time; I was nervous but excited. After what felt like ages, a messenger boy came looking for me and told me to follow him to the interview room. I asked if there were many applicants.

'Twenty-five applicants were shortlisted over the last two days, and you are the last person they're interviewing.'

Entering the interview room, I was taken aback when I saw four people sitting across the table. I sat on my wet palms, trying to control my nerves.

'Hello, Gordon,' the personnel lady broke the ice. The other three were men; one had short hair, just like me. He was the oldest person on the panel and his name was Jack. Ollie had told me all about him; he was from a military background. Jack was head of security and in charge of the post room.

'We're looking for someone who can follow in the footsteps of our previous messenger boys. You will be expected to meet and deal with all kinds of artists and famous people, some of which can be very difficult. You'll deliver the post, work long hours; you'll do shift work at weekends as required and finally, you'll have to wear a uniform and look smart at all times. Is that acceptable to you, Gordon?' The woman continued and I nodded profusely, showing I didn't mind what I did; I just wanted the job!

'Why television, Gordon? What got you interested?' asked one of the men.

'I've always liked music and television. My father works in the theatres in the West End, and I got to know and understand the business by joining him at work on my school holidays. I've learnt a lot at the theatres and I believe television is different but works in a very similar way.'

More questions ensued, mostly about television. I answered the questions confidently and professionally but with a sense of humour that made the interviewers smile and laugh. The interview seemed to be coming to an end when the woman took over proceedings, asking about my age and schooling.

'You are the youngest person to apply for this job. Why did you decide to leave school so soon?'

'Ma'am, I believed that practical experience would be better for me than staying on at school. I feel strongly about what I want to do in life – I want to work in the television industry, and I knew that school wouldn't prepare me for that,' I replied.

The panel nodded as I finished. The Head of Administration then added, 'We were looking for a more mature person. You do seem rather young to be starting a full-time job. Would you not consider coming back to apply in a year or two?' I sensed there was concern about my age and could feel the opportunity slipping away.

'I came for an interview last year but there was a mix-up and I didn't get an interview at all. The man told me to come back this year. So this is actually my second attempt for the job.'

They looked at each other, and the lady asked, 'Is there anything else you would like to add before we end the interview?'

I had only one last chance to convince them I was the right person for the job.

'I know I look rather young; I can't help this baby face,' I said with a big grin which got a little smile from the panel, 'but I am very mature for my age, and I know exactly what I want to do. If you ask any of the pensioners from the hard of hearing club, where I help out every Tuesday, they'll tell you that I'm mature for my age. Two years ago, without me knowing, they entered my name into the London evening newspaper competition for 'Teenager of the Year'. Over a hundred pensioners sent letters and I became a runner-up for the award!'

The panel seemed impressed. More questions were asked about the specifics of my involvement with the pensioners, which I answered eagerly.

'Do you have the newspaper letter on you?' asked the Head of Administration.

I produced the letter from the evening newspaper. The panel started to whisper amongst themselves and then looked at me.

'Normally we like to discuss the outcome of the interviews after we have seen everybody. Since you're the last candidate to be interviewed, we feel we can make our decision right now. Can you start on Monday morning?'

My jaw dropped; I was lost for words. But only for a second.

'Yes, yes; I can start on Monday, no problem!' I said, almost tripping over my words in excitement.

My social work for the hearing-impaired pensioners over the last six years had paid off; that's what I called good karma.

Instead of going back to the photographer's studio, I decided to share this brilliant news with Bill. I knew where to find him: having his liquid lunch in his favourite pub off Oxford Street, The Angel. I deliberately walked in with the saddest face I could muster and I told Bill and his friend, Mick, that I didn't get the job.

'Bill, you were right; my face didn't fit. No luck with the job,' I said, almost a little too theatrically. Bill didn't catch on.

In his best comforting voice he said, 'Don't worry

about it, Gordon, you still have a job at the photography studio.'

'Ha! Got you. My face does fit, Bill. I got the job; I start this Monday!'

Bill was ecstatic and bought a round of drinks for everyone to celebrate.

I still had to go back to the photography studio and to tell the boss I would be leaving. The secretary saw me coming and sighed, waving me towards the door as she handed me my pay packet for the week. She didn't even ask me what I wanted.

When the boss heard me coming, he started to shout at the top of his voice, 'No! Not you again! What is your problem? How dare you come into my office again looking for another pay rise?'

His hands were up in the air and his face was reddened with anger. It looked as if he might explode at any second.

'I'm not looking for any increase, Mr Ware,' I said in a gentle voice. He sat back on his seat and deflated slightly. I could see he was relieved.

'I'm handing in my notice. I'm leaving the job.'

'What, you're resigning?'

'Yes, I got another job at LWT Studios, Mr Ware. It all happened today. They're paying five times what you pay me, with expenses for travel and food on top. I start on Monday morning.'

You went for an interview in my time? You'll regret leaving, mark my words. You haven't given two weeks' notice so let me have that pay packet you just collected'

I put the money on his table.

'And last week's money?'

'Oh, I've spent that.' I replied.

'Well, you must work another week before you leave. Forget about your new job, you still work for me.'

'I've resigned. I'm not coming back!' I said, quickly exiting his office. I picked up my jacket and ran down the stairs. Mr Ware tried following me but it was impossible due to his weight. He lumbered a few steps outside the building before having to stop.

'Come back, you rogue! You can't leave, I want my money back!' he howled after me.

'Goodbye!' I shouted, giving a cheeky wave from a safe distance away as I ran down the street to catch my bus home.

Chapter Six

It's a Man's World

'You're one lucky boy, Gordon. Someone's looking out for you,' Mum said when I told her the news of my new job. I had one of the most joyful weekends ever, basking in the knowledge I would be starting work for London Weekend Television Studios on Monday. The world really was my oyster. I spent this blissful weekend with a woman named Sophia. My cousins, Nellie and Denis, had introduced me to an unusual Irish housewife named Terri who was famous in the Greek Cypriot community for fortune telling. More often than not, there would be a queue of people outside her north London home waiting to have their tea leaves read. It was here at Terri's where I met Sophia. I was intrigued by this mysterious psychic world and eager to explore it, perhaps because of the immense boredom of the basement job. Terri would teach me how to read tea leaves and tell me outrageous stories. I could never work out whether they were true or not, but that was all part of the fun. I was just totally captivated by her aura of mystery, possibly because of her gypsy blood.

There were other forces, however, drawing me into Terri's psychic world. Sophia was a Greek Cypriot in her thirties. She was about my height, but when she put on her high heels she towered above me. She was very funny and had a gorgeous Mediterranean face; big brown eyes and a fit body which she flaunted in her tight and revealing clothes. She took a shine to me, which helped to take my mind off the horrible job in the basement. I was quite smitten myself, and she was the first older woman I fancied. She often invited me to have dinner and dance with her in Greek clubs in north London, which usually ended up at her place. I'd had many sexual encounters with both boys and girls of a similar age to me beforehand, but I learnt a lot from this captivating mature woman.

Mum did not approve of me spending time with these two women. She was a little concerned I was going to be led astray by them. I didn't tell her half of the other things I got up to or she would have had heart failure. It was much safer to keep what I did in my free time to myself.

My weekend with Sophia, before starting the job at LWT, was a symphony of endings and beginnings.

'I'm so pleased about your new job, Gordon. But you must move on with your life now and make the most of this opportunity. Take this as a parting gift and remember the time we spent together,' she said as she handed me a bottle of Brut 33, my favourite fragrance at the time. She sent me away with a kiss; it was a bittersweet moment as I really enjoyed being with Sophia but we both knew it was time to move on.

On Monday morning, I arrived at the LWT studios in Ollie's car to start my new venture as a sixteen-year-old messenger boy. Ollie had been driving for about a year as he finally passed his driving test after many failed attempts, however I still felt nervous being in his car. He told me a lot about the studios and what to look out for along the way.

'You have to join the union, Gordon. Otherwise the studio people won't work with you.' I hadn't realised how unionised the television business was until that moment.

I made my way to the post room; it was 7.30 am and I was half an hour earlier than I needed to be. Opening the door, I met another messenger boy, called Steve, in his grey military-type uniform with a black stripe down the side of his trousers; his hair was longer than mine. I wasn't sure what he thought of my very short hair, which

I had just cut again over the weekend. My boss, Jack, walked in. He was also wearing a uniform and spoke in a military fashion, which I found quite amusing.

'Steve, show Gordon the ropes, and get your hair cut by this weekend if you want to keep your job! Look at Gordon's hair; short, neat and tidy. Don't let them influence you, Gordon, and end up with this!' he said as he swiped his hand through Steve's hair. 'I'll be keeping an eye on you!'

I was one of four messenger boys. The internal and external post had to be delivered and collected on time, every few hours, from the young secretaries who were constantly typing away.

There was a radio in the back of the post room which meant I could listen to music all day. James Brown's enormous hit, 'It's a Man's World' was playing and I sang along while sorting out the post. From the first day I worked in television, I found that it was indeed a white man's world; they held all the important positions in the company. It was uncommon to have women producers or studio directors in late 1969. Only in the make-up and wardrobe departments would you see a woman's name posted on the door as head of department.

Men were paid considerably more money than women. Equality between the sexes did not exist. The entire studio crews, from cameramen to technicians, were men. The creative side was also male dominated, though women fought hard to break into this closed shop. Men talked down to women and it was reflected in everyday interactions in the studios; 'When you've finished, can you go make the coffee? And don't forget to pop out and get me my cigarettes and the evening newspaper before you go.'

Only a small group of women moved up the television ladder; they had to work exceptionally hard for a position. There was, however, one very important job for women in television: the production assistant, or 'PA'. She would shadow the directors during the build-up to the pre-production and studio recording days. Her job was critical in the making of programmes. She was usually the first to arrive in the morning and the last to leave at night and you would find she knew more about making productions than the directors or producers at times! And yet in spite of their crucial roles, the PA's took plenty of verbal abuse from some of the more egotistical directors, who had a self-imposed God like presence. Seeing a woman cry as she tried to do her best in the glamorous world of television was not nice.

Many of the directors who worked at the studios had big personalities and unpredictable behaviour. The studio crews could be very creative in awarding them unflattering nicknames such as 'Mr Paranoid', 'Little

Hitler' and 'Fuck Anything that Moves'. These were just some the names for the straight directors. As for the gay ones, girls' names and derogatory pseudonyms like 'Fat Mary', 'Evil Queen', 'Ugly Witch', 'Bitch' and 'Cocksucking Whore' were popular.

I would observe directors going about their work, believing that one day I would be one of the producers working alongside them. The majority of them wanted to be admired and loved, just like the artists they worked with. Rivalries between directors was to be expected; men could be bitchier about each other than women. And I'm not just talking about the gay men; the straight men were just as bad!

My job was tremendously varied; I was in my element. If I worked overtime, I would get paid double time. To me, it never felt like work. It felt more like a holiday camp where I was being paid to learn all about the industry, the personalities and how everything works. I had the time and the freedom to roam about the five studios, talking to everyone while proudly wearing my new uniform, watching how the studios operated. In the evenings, we would receive a list of names of the guest artists arriving at the studios for the next morning.

My early shift meant going into the dressing rooms before the cleaners arrived. You could easily imagine the shenanigans of the night before based on the state of the room. Especially regulars like the legendary comedian and magician, Tommy Cooper, who loved a drink and left numerous empty bottles in his dressing room. Sometimes the dressing rooms became party venues for the artists and their entourage. On many occasions, I found people sleeping in the rooms or even having sex. It wasn't just the artists bending the rules; the LWT staff also used the dressing rooms and other areas in the studios for intimate moments. I saw many red faces in my first year.

Well-known politicians, stars and celebrities from the world of music would arrive at the studios every day. I was always happy escorting the pop stars I idolised, like Cher and the Bee Gees, to their dressing rooms.

'Who did you see at the studios today, Gordon?' Mum would ask.

'Tom Jones!' I just knew how to get her excited. Tom was her favourite.

'Ah, is he nice? What song was he singing? Did you get his autograph for me?' She was as thrilled as I was with the comings and goings at the studios.

'Oh Mum, I can't ask for autographs. I don't want to look star-struck or something.'

'Okay, okay; just asking. Don't want you to look silly or anything. Why don't you invite Tom over for a bit of home-cooking next time you see him?'

I would have loved to get Tom's autograph for Mum,

but we had been explicitly told not to ask for autographs from the guests.

In addition to the studios and offices, there were many other areas like a carpenter's workshop, a metal workshop, lighting and props rooms, film editing suites and transmission areas. There were so many elements that made up the studios. I took as long as I could to deliver the post in order to feed my desire to learn and understand more about the industry. I could be in the props room picking up something and take the opportunity to ask questions over a cup of tea. I was renowned for being a good listener, and people went out of their way to be helpful and give advice.

Jack would pop into the post room every so often and his first question to the boys would be, 'Where's that bloody Gordon? Is he not back yet? Must be talking with everybody in the bloody studios again.' And he was right.

Everybody got to know me, from the cleaners to the managing director. I was using all the charm skills I'd learnt from one of Mum's laundry drivers, Alf the Flirt. He introduced me to the word 'charm', and what a great favour he did for me! His lessons and guidance helped me get what I wanted, most of the time.

Messenger boys were asked to attend to the demands of the artists, and we would take it in turns to go and see the likes of Frankie Howard, the popular comedian. He was just one of many artists who took a shine to us; we would just laugh it off, seeing the funny side.

One day I was in the main studios watching the brilliant Tommy Steel, who had many hit records. He was Britain's answer to Elvis Presley in the 1960s. David Bell was a talented television director and was making a music special with Tommy. They were working on a major dance routine with thirty dancers. David was famous for his wicked Scottish sense of humour and could be very camp at times. He called me over from the side of the studio; 'I need you do something for Tommy and me. You can dance, can't you?'

'Yes, but not like those professionals over there.'

But before I knew it, I was told to do a stand-in for Tommy in the middle of the studio floor. The spotlight was on me while the rest of the studio was in darkness. The music started playing and within seconds, I was surrounded by twenty professional dancers. All of a sudden, they threw me around like a rag doll while the studio crew watched, in fits of laughter. The experience left me in a dizzy state of shock, however I received a great round of applause from the studio crew on the floor. Being a double for Tommy was fine, but I knew my future would be behind the camera, not in front of it.

Drugs like 'uppers', a stimulant for keeping you going, and 'downers', for slowing you down, were commonly taken in the studios at the time. I remember one of the electronic engineers, who looked like Jesus Christ with his long hair and sandals, giving me my first joint when I was almost eighteen.

'Try this; you'll be transported into another world. It's great!'

I went back to the post room on a high, laughing for the rest of the day and ended up sleeping it off in there. That was the first and the last time I tried drugs. They really weren't my thing.

The studio staff loved nothing better than gossip; it was the entertainment business after all. The messenger boys were renowned for being the first to hear and see what was going on around the studios. We knew almost everybody and would receive invitations to many parties and get-togethers outside of work. These events were the source of many exaggerated stories circulating around the studios.

'I hear the messenger boys were dancing naked in cages with male dwarfs and all,' was just one of the many outlandish stories. I put it all down to the gay 'queens' fantasising and creating gossip to see how far it might spread. The studios had indeed become my new playground.

One day, a letter arrived from the local council informing us that our little rented house in north London was to be demolished and we were to be moved to a new council estate known as Broadwater Farm in Tottenham. I was not happy as I loved our home. When I told Mum and Bill about my negative feelings towards large council estates, they were surprised. They had never been to a council estate and for them, there seemed to be more benefits than drawbacks.

'We'll have central heating and a proper bathroom, which means no more washing in the sink. You must admit, it's going to be a big improvement from a damp house with only electric fires to keep us warm,' said my mum, excitedly.

I delivered papers to council estates and occasionally I would visit my friends who lived in them. Some council estates were nice; they were usually the smaller ones. But there were many larger ones that seemed to be quite scary. If you were in any way astute, you would not want to live in them. From the moment we moved to Broadwater Farm, which was a huge estate with twelve tall, concrete tower blocks and endless long open corridors, you could never be sure who might be lurking around one of the many corners. There were over one thousand dwellings in this concrete jungle; it was one of the biggest council estates in the country.

After a couple of years as a messenger boy, I had worked out which department I wanted to work in when the opportunity arose. It was known as the VTR (Video Transfer Recording) department; it covered transmission, editing, and recording of programmes. I could learn all about the post-production and transmission side of the business. There was only a small group of well-paid individuals who worked in the department, all of which were men, and I made it a point to get close to them. Soon I was invited to watch the editing of shows. Not long after that, I got a job as an assistant in the library of the department; I was over the moon.

The department had a reputation for threatening strikes, which meant the loss of advertising money: the lifeblood of television. The management usually closed deals with influential unions to avoid any confrontation and disruptions. Each time there was a threat of strikes, my wages were raised. I had always wanted a sports car and I was soon able to buy a second-hand white MGB GT. My first sports car. I drove the car to work with Curtis Mayfield's, 'Move on Up' blasting through the stereo.

The television union's overtime payments were outrageous; four or five times the regular hourly rate. After two years in the job, I had enough money to buy my first home. When I told Mum about moving out and buying my own flat, she was astounded but very pleased for me. Owning my own home was very important to me. I put it down to not seeing the inside of a house until I was almost nine years old. Having never lived in a home that we owned, it felt like something I had to prove to myself.

'You're doing the right thing, Gordon. You'll need your own space to get on with your life. Bill and I will be fine here.' Although I didn't want to acknowledge it because of the enormous guilt, I knew Mum shared my dream; she would have loved Bill to have been able to afford a small house.

Working in the VTR department, I got to know the studio directors and producers (also known as the 'Gods') a lot better. I was driven to progress through the production teams and then move on to become a producer as fast as possible. I was impatient and didn't want to spend years climbing the slow ladder within the studio system.

Television was changing fast; only a few directors stood out and they were mostly freelance. Mike Mansfield was already ahead of the game. He was an unsuccessful actor who became a television director instead, which he took to like a duck to water. He had his own distinctive pop and rock look, including long white hair that he flicked a lot, which made him stand out from the crowd. He only ever wore jeans and the top two buttons of his shirt were always left undone. You could say he created a look for himself, like the many music artists he worked with.

He wanted not only to be a director, but a recognised personality on screen. I got to know him from my time sitting in the editing suites, and he knew I wanted to get into productions.

So, you want to work in light entertainment? You're into music? You must meet David Deyong, my business partner, and producer. Are you Jewish?'

The entertainment world had a strong Jewish presence, from agents to managers, and somehow they always had their finger on the pulse. Mike wasn't Jewish but David was, and they came together to make music videos for the latest songs. They were the first to do this commercially, offering the service to the record companies. Mike directed and David produced. They had no competition.

'I'm going to direct a live concert for Rod and his record company. Would you like to see how it is done?' Mike asked one day, to my great delight. I had been a big fan of Rod Stewart and the Faces since my school days.

With the success of the music video business, David, the deal maker, had devised and created a new music show with Mike, called Supersonic. It was a highly visible music show with Mike in the production gallery cueing the pop and rock stars. Mike and David retained the international television rights to sell the programmes; a new ground-breaking way of making television shows in a co-production deal. However, within weeks, David became ill and Mike informed me he was not going to live for long. He invited me to have a drink with him.

'I'd like to offer you a production assistant job working on Supersonic. You'll need to go freelance. You will be expected to do everything from making tea to exporting the Supersonic shows overseas. Be prepared to work long hours; you won't get paid overtime, but if the show works, you'll have a good paying full-time job. Are you in?'

This was literally a dream come true; his proposal was music to my ears. I wanted to share my news with Mum and Bill. When I got home, however, only Bill in the house.

'Bill, I have great news for you. I've decided to move into the fast lane; I'm leaving the LWT Studios and going freelance next week.'

'What! Are you sure? Leaving your good job for a thirteen weeks contract? I think you're crazy,' Bill exclaimed. He was naturally cautious when making big decisions in life, so I'm sure my sudden change of direction was a source of great anxiety for him.

'It is a risk, Bill, but better than waiting ten years to become a producer. Don't worry. If it doesn't work out, I'll rent out my new flat and come back to live with you and Mum,' I said, in an attempt to calm him. Not that I wanted to move back home; I was enjoying my independence far too much.

Bill didn't know what to say.

The main topic of conversation over the next Sunday lunch was, of course, my decision to join Mike.

'Let the boy do what he thinks is right, Bill. He's been right so far with all of his decisions. Have some confidence in him. I'm sure he'll do well in his new adventure,' Mum finally intervened. Bill relented and the conversation meandered towards other subjects.

Around that time, Mum also had a change of employment. She left the job in the laundry to work in a new local supermarket on the council estate. She thought having a job closer to home would make life easier, but I wasn't too pleased about it. I didn't say anything though. It had been a few years since Mum and Bill moved into Broadwater Farm and petty crime had arrived with a vengeance. It started with cars being broken into. Then burglaries increased. The residents who lived in or near the estate were worried about the increase in crime and began moving away. Strangers and gangs came from elsewhere to sell drugs; it seemed like nowhere inside the estate was safe.

Chapter Seven
Smoke and Mirrors

The next stage of my life as a freelance Production Assistant was like a roller-coaster ride. It was September 1975; I had just turned twenty-one and I thought I knew what I was doing as I moved into another part of the entertainment world. From the outside it seemed very professional, but perhaps I was a little naïve.

From the first morning I arrived at the Supersonic office, I was answering the phones that never stopped ringing. There was only Mike, his PA and the freelance stage manager, David Matthews, in the production team. Mike rarely answered the phone; he was a God within the entertainment world and people were constantly hoping to talk with him. I was the most junior member of staff there, and it was a little nerve-wrecking to be dropped in the deep end of what can only be described as a mad house.

'Is that Mike? Can I talk with Mike? I know him from the past; we were great friends. Tell him I called.' It seemed like everybody was Mike's best friend; he had more best friends than anyone I knew!

The calls were always the same. Some guy boasting about his great new band or singer and how they were going to have a massive hit record. Very soon people I didn't know knew my name.

'Gordon, can you tell Mike about my record, please. Please get him to call me back.' These people were more than desperate to get their music acts onto his new show. You could hear it in their voices, and Mike had complete power to make it happen.

Records arrived in the office on the hour, every hour. Music people turned up unannounced to drop off their new records, all in the hope that Mike would be interested or could spare a few minutes to talk with them. I thought that I was street-smart, but now I was dealing with some of the biggest hustlers in the business. Endless bullshit poured down the phones. I could talk bullshit, but these guys were professionals.

Record companies, agents and managers were all after one thing: exposure. They would prostitute themselves to get it. With only limited television channels, the BBC and ITV music entertainment shows could facilitate the sale of records in the millions, making big bucks. Payola, as it was known, was a common monetary incentive paid to radio producers and DJs to get records played. It was illegal but widespread across the country.

The record companies' executives and promotion teams had whopping great budgets to entertain in the hope of getting their acts on television and radio. Eating out at the most fashionable, expensive restaurants; going to high-profile events and exclusive clubs was all part and parcel of how things were done. Going into this job, I had thought everything would be about the music. However I quickly learnt that it was actually all about the money and the record sales. Exposure was key in the music business in order to generate record sales. Beautiful female and handsome male 'escorts' of all sexualities would also be laid on with limos and Rolls Royce's collecting the guests to ferry them around, waiting until the early hours to take them home again. The music business was very much about smoke and mirrors.

Another part of this façade was the drugs. It was the icing on the cake for many people. 'How about something special to get you going?' was a typical line heard in the recording studios, clubs, and the entertainment offices. 'I have some of the best stuff from America.' Like the limos, it was all laid on for free to create the image of an exciting, party fuelled lifestyle.

This was an alien world hidden away from the general public. Some artists and managers would insist in the contracts that drugs had to be supplied, but the word 'drugs' was never used. It was replaced with flowers or limos to cover-up. Everyone within record companies knew about drugs but they turned a blind eye. I was always happy to indulge in the food and drink but never the drugs.

I had first encountered drugs when I started my nightclub. The older kids used to be into speed but all I could see were the terrible side effects. Gerard Greene and his brothers, Brian and Kevin had been my best friends since we went to the pictures every Saturday morning as kids. But Gerard got into heroin when he was nineteen and his life was completely ruined. I lost a dear friend and this exposure made me extremely wary of drugs and substance abuse.

When I joined Mike's production company, Glam Rock music and the Scottish Tartan ruled. Scotland's Bay City Rollers were the biggest selling boy band in the UK. The Rollers were selling more records than any other artists in America and the rest of the world. The devoted girl fans dressed like their idols, all in tartan. The other big names of the time were Garry

Glitter, Suzi Quatro, Showaddywaddy, Mud, Sweet, Alvin Stardust, David Essex, Status Quo, Bryan Ferry and Roxy Music.

Mike's style involved combining multi-camera direction, with five or more cameras, and the use of anything from wind machines and smoke machines, to foam, confetti and fireworks. Anything that created visual impact while the artists mimed to their songs was all the rage. With his distinctive style, Mike created a new look for music on television which placed his direction in even higher demand.

As a young production assistant, I was expected to meet artists at the studios to 'kill time' if Mike wasn't ready for them. Over drinks, I soon got to know regulars like Cliff Richard and Marc Bolan. Marc, also known as T. Rex, was a real flirt with both the guys and girls. His bisexual chat-up lines were very funny.

'So, Gordon, when are we going to have a night out together, huh? Are you dating? Girls? Or are you into boys? Come on, you can tell me. Your secret's safe with me. What are you doing later after the show? Let's go out and party!'

Meeting artists became second nature to me. I was never anxious and was always enthusiastic and friendly. However you never knew who your real friends were; many of them were hoping for favours in return. I learnt this quickly enough.

Supersonic was a great success and was extended for more shows. My contract was made permanent and I could carry on paying my mortgage, which was a huge relief. By the second year I already had a very good understanding of how the music business worked, but I was still learning and watching all the time. I saw the high side and the low side of the world of entertainment. I was meeting the likes of the Osmond Brothers and David Cassidy from the Partridge Family television series. He was already a big international television star with heaps of hit record sales. His success had started early as a young teenager. He was only four years older than me and already fed up with fans chasing him all over the world. He envied my life, which I found intriguing.

'I just wish I could walk down the street like anybody else with people not knowing who I am. I'm never out of the public eye; they always want a piece of me. I'm expected to hide my bad moods or personal difficulties. It never stops. It can be very lonely living out of hotels, always traveling and I'm sick of this lifestyle,' he said.

The price of fame and success; I saw this repeatedly with many young artists, wanting the success but then not knowing how to deal with it when it arrived. Fame is like a drug; they couldn't live without it, even when it became almost impossible to live with. Many turned to alcohol and drugs as a way of coping. Losing their celebrity status because of poor record sales became a common occurrence which was incredibly demoralising. The career span of the average pop star could be very short but that was the ruthless nature of the music business.

Mike was now known as 'Mr Pop' within the television and music business; he was as famous as the stars on his shows. He loved the celebrity status hosting Supersonic brought him, and linking the television control room to the studio with his celebrated trademark line, 'Cue the music' became a catchphrase everyone recognised.

When people saw him walking down the street they would call out to him, mimicking his tagline; 'Cue the music! Cue the music!'

Mike had the power to influence over five million people who watched Supersonic every week. Television was the main pastime of the nation and record sales were in the millions as youngsters went out to purchase the singles they heard on the show.

David Matthews, the stage manager for the production, was a fascinating guy to work with. He was incisive, knowledgeable and laid back. I don't think a week went by where I didn't find myself asking him for advice on something. He wasn't into pop or rock but loved theatre and opera. Whenever Mike changed his mind, which he did a lot, it was always David who delivered the bad news. Mike only liked to deliver the good news. This was common with many directors.

Every week, a production meeting would be held for the next show. The key studio people would arrive, including the senior cameraman, sound man; graphics and lighting directors and set designer. Mike's only female member of the team, his PA, would be making notes throughout the meeting. Each record would be played over and over to work out the visual ideas with the team. It was very amusing to see straight men camping it up with their ideas, becoming more animated. If you didn't know they were straight men, you might have thought they were all gay. I learnt a lot of gay lingo from these meetings.

It was fun and games at work, most of the time. But the social side after work was more than fantastic. Successful artists and music businesspeople would hang out at West End clubs most nights of the week, at the expense of the record companies and Mike. I soon developed a taste for champagne and mixed with the likes of Elton John, Rod Stewart and the new up-and-coming artist, Freddy Mercury. A far cry from the days of hanging out in the Irish pubs, waiting for paddies to buy me drinks.

It was a busy afternoon when a call came in from Billy Gaff, one the hottest managers in the music business. He was excited about his new signing, an American singer-songwriter called John Cougar, and wanted two videos made. His other artist, Rod Stewart, was having great success as a solo act after leaving the Faces.

'Gordon, if you're free why not come along to a Christmas party at my home? What part of Ireland are you from?' he asked in his soft Irish accent.

Parties and launch events for artists were plentiful, occurring almost on a daily basis; it was all about networking. It was impossible to attend them all so I only chose the ones that I thought would be fun and interesting.

I arrived with Mike at Billy Gaff's beautiful home. Rock stars, managers and media people were all there. It was a who's who music industry party to celebrate Rod Stewart's success with his first solo album in the charts after leaving the Faces. He was now living in LA with his new girlfriend, Britt Ekland. In one corner, a small group of powerful men, the gay mafia I called them, chatted amongst themselves. Their creativity and management skills followed in the style of the late Brian Epstein who managed the Beatles. The group consisted of Billy Gaff and Elton's manager, John Reid from Glasgow's working class who was renowned for his hot temper and being tough like a street fighter. Also present was another Scotsman, Tam Paton, the Bay City Rollers' manager. Mike joined them for drinks while I walked around the place, looking out for familiar faces.

I got myself a glass of champagne and watched the goings-on around me until I spotted a few people I knew and made my way to speak to them. There was a fantastic atmosphere with an abundance of great food and drink. After an hour there, however, I sensed a fight was brewing. I looked over to Mike who was looking rather happy and tipsy; he really couldn't hold his drink. Elsewhere I could hear an argument above the loud music. Then there was the crash of glass breaking. I had a horrible feeling things were about to go sour. I rushed over and pushed Mike in the direction of the front door.

'What are you doing, Gordon? Stop pushing me!'

'Just keep moving towards the door, Mike. Things are about to get nasty.'

Just as we left, the house filled with screams and shouts, and more sounds of breaking glass.

A few days later, the news got back to me that somebody had put a broken bottle in the face of a very well-known person. This was another side of the music business that the public didn't see; rough, revolting, intimidating and violent.

The world of music, and indeed music videos, was transformed when the band, Queen, released 'Bohemian Rhapsody'. It was a long song, six minutes, which was most unusual. Bruce Gowers, the director, revolutionised the music video in a way nobody had seen before with a unique style of direction. Very soon everybody was talking about his video which was shown over and over on television as the song remained in the number one spot for nine weeks.

One day I bumped into Bruce, who I knew from my days working as a messenger boy when he had just started directing in light entertainment. I hadn't seen him for a long time, and he told me he had just gone freelance.

'You must be enjoying yourself. That was a great break you got, working with Mike. Or should I say Mary,' he joked.

Mary was Mike's nickname within the business. I laughed and agreed with him.

Mike saw me chatting with Bruce and told me impatiently that he needed me; the rivalry between them was still very much alive and kicking.

Christmas was a very interesting time too. Gifts would start to arrive for Mike, from the finest and most expensive champagnes such as Cristal, Krug and Dom Perignon, to bucket loads of spirits, wines and the best chocolates. Every day I would have to go down to the reception to meet people bringing Christmas presents and hoping to meet Mike. Unfortunately for them, they only ever got to meet me.

'Happy Christmas, Gordon! I've got a great new record coming out in the New Year, any chance I can meet Mike and play him the song? I only need a few minutes.'

My standard reply when accepting the gifts was, 'Mike's in the studio and working late tonight, but I'll tell him you came. Thank you for the presents.'

I too received my share of presents; maybe they were thinking it was a way to get to Mike. I was very happy to play along regardless.

However when Elton John's manager, John Reid, called and wanted to know if Mike could do a video for a new single, 'Don't go breaking my heart', with Elton and Kiki Dee, it was a different matter. John said it was urgent and wanted to speak with Mike there and then. When I told him that Mike was in the studio doing a Rod Stewart television special and could not be interrupted, he shouted in his strong Glaswegian accent, 'I know Phyllis is doing her fucking special, that's why I need to talk with Mike about doing a fucking video right now.'

'Sorry, but who is Phyllis?' I asked.

'It's Rod's nickname, you fucking dumb wit, just get

Mary on the phone! Now!' Mike took the call and the video was made. The song became Elton's first number one in the charts.

Compared to the 'outside world', the entertainment industry somehow allowed people to be themselves in terms of their sexuality. David Bowie led the way with his colourful gender-bending lifestyle, which he made no attempt to conceal, and made bi-sexuality acceptable. People in the industry talked about being straight or gay but, from my experience, there were more bisexual than gay people. I knew that I was bisexual and met my fair share of people with similar persuasions. Music people were always worried about referring to their artists as 'gay' as it was considered not to be good for record sales. Artists' sexuality was still kept in the confines of the people in the industry, even though there were rumours and speculations amongst the public. Around this time, the tabloid newspapers had something new to talk about: AIDS. When AIDS first surfaced, it was only associated with gay men. It had a devastating effect and caused a major setback for the community.

At this point, Supersonic looked as though it was set to continue but like all good things in life, it came to an end. Mike felt dejected; he didn't see the change in the music scene. Glam Rock was out, and Punk Rock was in. Punk made the past music scenes look tame. Record companies, music producers and managers could sometimes be very slow in identifying the winds changing within the music business.

During my two years' working with Mike, I had never thought of taking a holiday. The job was a dream job but even then, I did not see myself working for Mike forever. I informed Mum and Bill that I might need to move on because Supersonic was over.

'You've learnt so much and met a lot of people. Surely you can find another job,' Mum said. She was right, but my real aspiration was to work for myself and have my own business.

In the same week, a new punk band called the Sex Pistols needed videos for 'God Save the Queen' and 'Pretty Vacant'. When I first met Malcolm McLaren, I thought he must be the lead singer for the Sex Pistols with his colossal ego and big mouth. So I was surprised to find out that he was actually their manager. In most cases, bands always need a leader and a frontman.

'I'm the man behind the Punk Revolution; I'm going to change the music scene and the world,' he told me and anybody who would listen to him. He may have talked a lot but the real person behind the punk look and the designs was his partner, Vivienne Westwood.

I took the band to get changed and for make-up.

John Lydon, who had an Irish background, was the lead singer and like most of the bands I met, was working class. The ITN news studios were hired for making the videos and had a no-alcohol policy. McLaren, however, had his own ideas as he handed out cans of lager to the other Sex Pistols that morning.

'Can you go easy on the drinks and don't drink in the studio, please?' I asked in the make-up room.

McLaren wasn't listening and soon the band were all over the place shaking cans of lager onto themselves and the studio television crew. The security men soon arrived and escorted McLaren and the band out of the studios. The band did come back the next day to finish the videos with the record company picking up the extra bills incurred. A few years later, McLaren ended up in front of the camera as a solo recording artist, which again did not surprise me. This was all part of the rock and roll world, and anybody could be famous, or infamous for that matter.

After Mike's business partner, David Deyong, passed away, he made David's wife, Susie, an associate producer on the productions. However, Susie had very little say in Mike's business decisions. In late-summer 1977, Mike came back from a short holiday in the South of France only to find that Susie had set up her own production company. He was speechless.

'How disloyal is that! She is going into competition

with me, Gordon, can you believe it? She'll never make it, you know.' Mike was theatrical, bordering on hysterical.

I wasn't surprised it happened; Mike was old-school when it came to women in television. The next day, Mike informed me he wanted me to take over Susie's role and do everything except for agreeing the budgets with the clients.

'Gordon, here it is; a wonderful opportunity for you to produce,' he told me.

Mike offered me the opportunity to be a producer but was not willing to give me a producer's fee. I didn't care about the money this time; it was another step closer to where I eventually wanted to be.

Chapter Eight

Opportunity Knocks

With my new producer's role, I could see first-hand how music videos were becoming an increasingly important marketing tool for new records released. To make a video stand out involved spending more money to create something new and different. This meant moving away from the simple performance video to add elements of storytelling, building sets and using special lighting to create atmosphere.

A&M Records wanted two video promos made for a new three-piece punk band called The Police. The songs were 'Can't Stand Losing You' and 'Roxanne'. I saw this as a great opportunity to talk with Mike about doing something different and asking for bigger budgets. Instead, Mike agreed to make two inexpensive performance videos for less than a thousand pounds each. The only memorable thing about the making of the videos was finding out that Sting's real name was the same as mine.

I knew that as long as Mike was in charge of the budget and negotiating with clients, I would not be able to implement or even try out my ideas. After The Police productions I could only talk with one person, David the stage manager, about my predicament. I told him how frustrated I felt with my new role.

'How do I tell Mike that I'm disappointed with the productions and the missed opportunity we had? I have fresh ideas and I'd like more responsibility for the entire shoot. I have already been approached by other directors to produce for them. Maybe it is time for me to move on.'

David understood where I was coming from and offered to talk to Mike. I don't know what David said to Mike, but it was agreed I would be given a free hand in the budgets and negotiations.

I soon made myself busy developing closer relationships with the artists' managers. Knowing that record companies' marketing departments always wanted to spend as little as possible, I needed to get the managers to believe in spending more to ensure success for their artists.

Colin Johnson, Status Quo's manager, was the first

person I persuaded to look at bigger budgets. He was convinced I was right and agreed to my idea of shooting three videos at the same time for the album 'Rocking all over the world'. The budget went from being a typical few hours in the studio to a full-blown three-day shoot which required sets to be built and post-production editing. Colin made it all possible because of his pulling power with the record company. The videos were a huge success, helping record sales move into the millions. With the release of the first video, the phones in the office started ringing like crazy. Within the first month, Mike's earnings shot up. It was a win-win situation for the artists and Mike.

In the past Mike had received very little discount, if any, on hiring studios and equipment. Without informing him, I put together new studio-hire deals with up to a thirty-five per cent discount. I knew this would be the best time to ask for a producer's fee from Mike.

'No, Gordon, no, you are asking too much!' Mike gasped in horror when I approached him with my request.

'I need a deal of some kind here, Mike. The discounts I'm getting will make you much bigger profits. I don't feel you're sharing the benefits I'm bringing to the company. The accounts tell the story.'

I stood my ground; I had proven myself to Mike and

had confidence in my achievements. If this meant that I had to leave, it wasn't a problem. However, Mike did increase my pay, but still he refused to give me a producer fee. He also offered me a ten per cent profit on the tape copying side of the business which, in his eyes, was not a great revenue earner. I asked for the deal to be in writing.

I personally believed the copying business could be massive. I moved up another gear to improve the business, realising the record companies paid little attention to this boring side of the work, instead leaving the badly paid secretaries to deal with it. I made it my business to make friends with all the secretaries at every record company, inviting them for lunch and drinks. I told them all about my copying services and how I could take the burden off their hands, giving them peace of mind.

'Just leave it to me; see it as a one-stop copying service.' This became my new standard line.

Soon they were receiving Christmas and Easter chocolates from me. Within a few months I needed extra staff to help with the expanding business. The profit share I got out of this copying business soon mounted up. Mike couldn't believe what I was pulling in and wanted to change the deal, but he backed off when I reminded him of the contract letter he had signed.

On the production side of things, I was getting more bullish by the day. All the hustling was like a challenge; it was a game that just came naturally to me. However I did work on the simple premise of securing repeat business with the artists by making sure they always got what they wanted. We made a video for a shy young woman from Wales and her song, 'It's a Heartache', which had been a big hit all over the world. We made a further fifteen videos for Bonnie Tyler as well as repeat videos for the Three Degrees, Prince Charles's favourite three-girl group.

I'll always remember a production that was invoiced in full, but the artist didn't show up. On that occasion, a crew of fifty people were waiting around for Elton John to arrive for his shoot. I received a call from David Croker, the managing director of Elton's record company, telling me that Elton had gone missing. He was very pissed off. A second call from David confirmed that Sharon, Elton's nickname given to him by Rod Stewart, was still in bed after having had a late night out. I suggested we did the video the next day, but this wasn't possible due to Elton's commitments.

By this time, Mike was having kittens; 'What are you going to do about the money, Gordon? We only got part of the money.'

This was a first for me; asking for money with no video to show for it. Mike was standing next to me when I called David Croker.

'Hi, David. Unfortunately, I haven't any good news

for you. We don't get any discounts for a no-show, so I must invoice you for the full amount.'

David immediately went ballistic down the phone line shouting and swearing non-stop. I just kept silent while he ranted.

'Are you listening, Gordon? Are you still there?'

I was holding the phone slightly away from my ear. Mike could hear David shouting and left the studio office. I calmly told David, 'If we don't get paid in full, David, we'll see you in court, okay?'

'F—'

Before I could hear the rest of his rant, I put the phone down on him. I told Mike what had happened.

'That's it, we will never get the second payment,' Mike said.

I saw this as an expensive game of bluff. I suspected David would call back and he did. Before he could say anything, I told him, 'David, please don't start shouting or I'll put the phone down on you again. This situation is not of our making nor is it our fault. Pure and simple, the star did not turn up. I still have to pay all the people who turned up for work.'

David did pay the invoice in full and later we became good friends, doing more business together. Putting down the phone on people became my trademark. I wasn't going to listen to anyone shouting and ranting; it was very common in this outrageous business.

In between the madness of my job, which I loved, I would make my way to see Mum and Bill at the weekend, for breakfast or a Sunday roast dinner together. I felt guilt-ridden for not seeing more of them because of work, even though I was living the dream.

Mum was a great inventive cook and turned simple ingredients into tasty meals. She made the perfect Sunday roast, never over-done, and served with all the accompaniments. We had come a long way from our days in the hostel where we mostly ate end cuts of the animal and offal! While visiting them, I would always stock their refrigerator with all kinds of meats and food stuff to make sure they had enough.

'Have some more lamb, Gordon?'

'Thanks, Mum, I will have just a little bit more.'

'That's the third helping, Gordon. Where do you put it? You eat like a horse!' Bill remarked jokingly.

'Well, you eat away and enjoy it! There's plenty more where that came from,' Mum chuckled as she lit a cigarette to accompany Bill who had already started smoking.

'Mum, you should both try giving up that horrible habit,' I said in between chewing. 'You know it isn't good for you.'

'Oh sure, I know it isn't good for me, but it's a habit I

am not ready to give up just yet, okay? They're my only luxury. I'm allowed one bad habit, aren't I, Gordon?'

With the money coming in from the new role and profit sharing too, I upgraded from my flat into a three-storey house in the same area. When Mum saw the inside of the house, she was amazed.

'How do you afford this, Gordon?' Even I had to pinch myself sometimes when I thought about how far we'd come from the old days in the Dublin hostel. Life was looking good all round for Mum, Bill and myself. I already had plans to surprise them with a fantastic summer holiday in Spain. That was until we received the bombshell news about Mum's cancer.

Chapter Nine

Little White Lies

The hospital had become Bill's second home, replacing the pub. He was already there when I arrived and I was about to give the best acting performance of my life. I had decided not to tell my mum about her cancer, all in the hope of keeping her alive as long as I could. Bill looked confused by my air of optimism.

'You're looking well today Mum.' I gave her a gentle kiss and held her hand.

'I'm happy you're here.' She then shocked me by gripping my hand, pulling me towards her and whispering, 'Let's be honest, Gordon,' – she stopped midway and started coughing. I looked over at Bill, guessing he must have gone against my wishes and told her about the cancer – 'they can't fool me. This is not real tea, more like weak dishwater; weak like me. Can you get me a fresh, strong cup, please?' she said with a smile.

'Mum, I forgot to mention I have some good news for you!'

'Oh really, I could do with some of that.'

'Yes, but the news comes with a request. You need to make me a promise,' I said as I returned with a strong cup of tea.

'Sure, Gordon. Anything for you. What's your good news? Come on, tell me!'

'I was thinking, Mum, when you're better and ready to leave the hospital, would you like to move nearer to me?'

'What? You managed to get a council flat exchange, Gordon?' she asked excitedly.

'No, not exactly. I'm going to buy you and Bill a small flat with a garden, near me. I'll start looking this weekend. But first you must promise me to get better.'

'Oh, Gordon, really? Can you really do that?'

Bill gave me a startled look; he was stunned by my suggestion as it had come of the blue.

'Yes, I can. But first the doctors will need to do an operation on you and then you'll need to take some medicine which is going to be tough on you.'

'Operate on me?' The fear was immediately evident in her voice and my heart ached.

'They found some lumps in your lungs and they want

to get them out.'

'Is that what's making me feel so tired?'

'Yes, once they're out, you'll start to feel stronger again.'

'When are they going do it?'

'Very soon, Mum. Later today.'

'That soon?'

'Remember, I need you to help me choose your new home.'

'Oh, Gordon, anything you choose is fine.'

I could see her eyes welling up. I wasn't sure if it was because she was happy with my good news or upset about what the doctors were about to do.

I somehow managed to keep up with the performance all the way through, but seeing her about to cry eventually got to me. I had to turn away and walk to the nurses' counter, pretending I needed something from them. I returned to Bill and Mum after I had composed myself.

'Bill Lewis, what do you make of this good news? Did you know he was going to do this? Trust Gordon to find a way to get us off that horrible estate.'

'Yes, it's wonderful news. He didn't mention anything to me. I'm as surprised as you are!' Bill answered nervously, still stunned by the whole situation.

'Oh, Gordon, you scoundrel. Surprising us yet again. Thank you, I promise you I'll get better soon. Now, I need another real strong cup of tea to celebrate. Bill, make yourself busy and fetch me one, please.'

I wasn't sure how I did it, but I had managed to deliver the news to Mum about her operation without her getting upset. She was completely overwhelmed with the prospect of moving to a new home after leaving the hospital. We seemed to have completely side-lined her major surgery, or perhaps it was her way of playing along with us so that we wouldn't get upset with what was about to happen.

Later, Bill and I went to have a drink in the pub while Mum was taken into surgery. 'Gordon, how are you going to buy another property? I know you can't afford it.' Bill was right; I had only just moved into my new home and I had used up all my savings. But the money had to be found somehow. Little was said that afternoon as I was deep in thought, trying to figure out how I could find the money to deliver my promise. Mum had brought me up to be a very positive person, now it was my turn to make her feel positive.

The operation went well, without any complications. Bill and I were relieved, and I started looking for a flat the day after the surgery. That was the easy bit. I went to see my friendly bank manager as he was always helpful.

'Sorry, our bank is not giving out second mortgages at the moment. The money market is very tight; but it might get better later in the year.'

I couldn't wait until then. I had to find another way to get the money. In one week, I had seen over thirty properties near my home. The one that I really liked and offered to buy was a first floor, one bedroom flat with a garden, owned by a local builder. He had run out of money to finish the work and was desperate to do some kind of a deal to get out of his mess. It was a good deal and I didn't see the lack of kitchen and fitted wardrobes as a problem. Now it was about finding the deposit and a mortgage to complete the deal. I was feeling more fraught with each passing day, and had no one to share my apprehensions with.

Mike's accountant had arrived in the office for his annual chat with Mike, but Mike was running late. While waiting, we talked over coffee about how good the video copying business was doing.

'I see your pay cheques getting bigger each month, Gordon,' he remarked, and I grinned.

'I feel the next step with the copying business would be to expand it; buy all the necessary equipment and a building to house it. With the profits that are coming in, it makes commercial sense, right?' I queried.

'Yes, buying a property for the business is tax efficient and financially beneficial for Mike' the accountant agreed.

I also told the accountant that I had tried to persuade Mike to take on an additional television director to help with the increasing amount of productions, hoping that he would also suggest it to Mike.

Mike arrived in a foul mood throwing his briefcase on his desk; there has been some kind of drama in his love life.

'Don't tell me Gordon is putting ideas into your head again?' Mike asked the accountant, knowingly.

We laughed and then the accountant mentioned my idea about the copying business and buying a building. Mike flicked his hair, then put his hands together with the tips of his fingers touching his chin, giving the impression he was thinking about it.

'Hmm, Gordon always has ideas. Always smelling the money. I'm sure he's an Irish Jew, you know.'

Mike found it funny poking fun, but the accountant was nodding his head at my suggestions. I excused myself and left them to continue talking. I treated Mike's business as if it was my own and he was more than content to let me make money for him.

The next morning, Mike wanted to have a meeting with me over lunch. This was his way of doing business, always over lunch or dinner. He was buzzing with excitement.

How do we set up an in-house copying business?

What equipment do we need? How much would it cost? What about staff?' The questions kept coming. Mike was impatient. 'I am going to make you very rich,' he said. 'Your profit share will go through the roof. I'm going to buy a commercial building; this will be a big investment for me. You had better deliver the goods, Gordon.'

'Don't you worry, Mike, I'll make it work for you.'

'Good to know. But since I'm investing this huge amount, I need you to sign a three-year contract with me.'

'Mike, I'm happy to sign this contract with you, but I'll need a lump of money upfront. Call it a loan if you want. I need to buy a flat or she'll die,' I said, suddenly welling up with emotion.

'Slow down, Gordon. Stop rabbiting on. Who's dying? What lump sum? Flat? I thought you just bought a new house' Mike interrupted.

I took a breath; 'It's my mum, Mike. She just had a major operation for cancer in the lung and she'll die if I don't buy her a flat and move away from that awful council estate she's in.'

'Oh, Gordon, you're so melodramatic, she is not going to die.'

My serious face said it all. Mike realised very quickly how much this meant to me.

'So how much do you need?'

'Eight thousand. With the profits from the copying business, I can pay you back in six to eight months.'

Silence. Mike took a minute to ponder.

'Okay, you sign a three-year contract and you can have the money.' He offered his hand to shake on it.

Three years felt like a lifetime to me, but I needed the money.

'Mike, no interest on the loan and you have your deal.' Mike nodded his head and I shook his hand.

Now I had a deposit, but I still needed a mortgage. Luckily, I found a broker who could provide a new kind of 'pension mortgage', which had higher monthly repayments. I worked out that I could just about maintain payments for the two mortgages. It was all going to be very tight.

When Bill saw the flat, his face lit up; he was speechless and got a little emotional; 'It's beautiful, Gordon. Cathleen is going to be so happy when she sees this.'

'Bill, it's only walls and central heating, it'll need quite a bit of work to make it perfect, especially with no kitchen and wardrobes.'

'Don't worry about the work; your Mum will love the flat by the time I've finished with it. Oh, that small garden will be great, we can grow our own vegetables.'

I decided to let Bill tell Mum the good news in hospital and I went off to sign the final papers for the property that afternoon.

Bill started the works immediately and four weeks later, Mum was ready to leave the hospital. Even though the flat was not finished, she insisted on going to live there rather than going back to Broadwater Farm. The moment she stepped into the flat she had tears rolling down her rosy cheeks. She was speechless; her hand over her mouth and her head shaking in disbelief as she walked around admiring Bill's handiwork. She later walked up to me and held my hands, her teary eyes looked straight into mine and she whispered, 'Thank you.'

I was so pleased to have been able to pull this off for my mum; she finally had her own home. In my eagerness to pursue my dreams, I forgot my mother had hers too. She had made many sacrifices to help make me the person I am, and finally I was giving her something she had always dreamt of in return; a home she could call her own.

After Mum moved into her new home, she was always beaming with joy and had a new lease of life. They both loved the small garden which brought so much pleasure. Bill and I were very pleased with Mum's progress but we were always worried she would suddenly leave us.

Not long after Mum and Bill moved from Broadwater Farm, riots erupted in the estate. A policeman, PC Keith Blakelock, was killed on the estate. It was the scene of some of London's worst riots and was a major news story on television and in newspapers all over the country. It was an experiment in high-density social housing which had failed miserably. It had been a disaster waiting to happen.

Meanwhile at work, Mike had fallen in love with another new guy, Andy, a cameraman. The new couple went off on a holiday to the South of France for a week. I always opened all the mail when Mike was away. The contents of one letter revealed that a new investor was to be joining our copying business, as an equal partner, and all the paperwork had been signed off. There was no mention of my ten per cent of shares in the business. The business was thriving and had made me enough money to pay back Mike's loan within less than six months.

That weekend I thought long and hard about the letter and what it meant for me. At first, I was very angry at being side-lined without a word or discussion. I already knew Mike wanted to please Andy who, since they got together, had been asking Mike to invest a substantial amount into buying camera equipment. I thought if Mike kept my shares, I could walk out with my last payment, and we would be quits.

On the Monday morning Mike arrived back into the office feeling refreshed and full of joy after his holiday. There was a real spring in his step as he walked into my office.

'Anything I need to know about, Gordon? Any new productions for me to do?' he asked, grinning like a Cheshire cat.

I was on the phone and so indicated I would speak to him later. After about ten minutes I confronted Mike in his office with the letter.

'Can you explain this?'

Mike looked at the letter. 'I meant to speak to you about this. Can we talk about it over dinner tonight?'

'No, Mike, you seem to have just sold my ten per cent of the business without even asking me.'

'I need to raise the money for my next investment, Gordon.'

'Okay, but I'm supposed to be your partner in the copying business.'

'Well, actually you don't hold any shares in the company formally.'

'Are you saying our signed agreement for the ten per cent of the shares doesn't mean anything? After all the work I did to make it successful?'

'Come on, Gordon, we can sort this out. Let's go through it over dinner.'

'I'll tell you what, you keep the shares. Yes, keep my shares,' I told him angrily.

'I'm pleased you're coming round. We can tie up the

loose ends with a new deal for you, I promise.'

'Mike, the only thing I want is the money outstanding to me. I'm done. I'm leaving the company now, today.' I said as I stood up and proceeded to walk out of the room. Mike jumped up from his chair and quickly followed me.

'Come on, Gordon. You've signed a three-year contract with me, you have over two years left.'

I stopped and turned around, staring at Mike squarely in the face with my finger pointing at him; 'You have the cheek to bring that up after you broke the business contract with me? Thank you for the break but it's time for me to move on.'

Mike was lost for words but carried on following me to the front door of the building.

'You can't go, Gordon!'

I kept walking before I changed my mind. Mike's actions had made it easy for me to leave his company. I just hoped he would honour the monies outstanding to me. It was a considerable amount, enough to pay the mortgages and my living expenses for another year or so.

Over the following week however, the worst of my fears came true as Mike refused to pay me unless I returned to work for him.

I did not go back.

Chapter Ten

Going for Broke

I had always wanted to work for myself, but I never thought I would leave Mike in the way I did. I had no time to think about taking a break as I had two mortgages to pay. I decided Mum and Bill must not know about my current situation as this would worry them and ruin their enjoyment of their new home.

I had always been good at delegating and finding people for making productions. First, I would need to find myself an assistant. I did have one young guy in mind, Mark. He was working for a film production company when I first met him a few months earlier at a television event; he mentioned he was looking for a new job to challenge him.

'The company I work for is trying to put together a major television deal but they're having problems with the economy. It's getting worse by the week. I have very little to do in the office as everything's on hold and it's bloody boring being there on my own,' he told me.

Mark had recently left university and felt like a glorified messenger boy. His company's main office was in the Pinewood Studios, outside London, but they retained a small office in central London next to Piccadilly Circus in anticipation of this television project. I phoned him to have a chat and arrived later the same day at his office.

'Wow! What a place you have here. Am I disturbing you?'

'Nah, just reading a book. Would you like a cup of tea or coffee?'

'The rent must be a fortune.'

'Don't know, mate. I don't pay the rent. I just sit about and answer the phones when they ring.'

I was there for about an hour, during which time the phones in his office never rang.

'Why are your phones not ringing?' I asked.

He chuckled and told me, 'Only when somebody from the main office wants something done would I get a call. I'll maybe have one call a day. Sometimes none at all.'

Mark was being completely wasted here; I took a second to consider what he had told me.

'Mark, how would you like to work for me?'

'For you? Anytime! That would be fantastic, when do

I start?!' he asked with eagerness.

'You can start right now. I'll need to use your office and phones, unofficially of course, until I can find myself an office. What do you think?'

'You are joking, right?' he asked, wide eyed with disbelief.

'No, if you want in, I'll need to use your office for a while. I can't pay you anything until I get my first commission so you'll need to stay in your current employment until I can pay you a salary.'

Still slightly bewildered, he nodded his head gently, slowly realising what I was asking of him. It was a wild proposition, but he came on board.

'May I?' I asked as I picked up the nearest phone, pulled out my black book with the names of my contacts, and started dialling.

Mark was short on experience, but he made up for it with a great attitude and embraced the new challenge that was coming his way.

'What do you have to lose? You don't like your job and were going to leave anyway,' I said to help solidify his decision. 'My company will be called GLO, Gordon Lewis Organisation, and I would like you to be my production assistant. Are you alright with that?'

Mark could only nod his head and laugh. I had infected him with my energy and enthusiasm. I gave him a list of phone numbers for some record companies and other contacts so he could try and set up meetings through the PAs and secretaries.

'Tell them you're working for me and that this is my new phone number, based in Piccadilly Circus.'

'This is possibly the most exciting thing to happen to me in the five months I've been in the business,' Mark remarked as he got started on the phone.

I started planning our get-out lines, just in case someone appeared in the office unexpectedly.

'If I'm in the office and anyone turns up, I will leave within seconds of their arrival. If the phones ring, you can pretend the incoming calls have the wrong number. No meetings will take place in the office.'

'Are you on drugs, Gordon?'

'Nope, just high on adrenaline.' All I could think of was a free office and no overheads.

I had a few things in mind for my company; making music videos and television programmes. Therefore my other important task was to find a new generation of young directors with great ideas, and fast. This, I knew, could be the hardest part of my job.

As soon as the word was out about me setting up my own business, I got approached by a number of directors. It would have been very easy for me to start poaching Mike's music clients. However, I had decided not to work with the artists from my past, with the music scene changing yet again.

It was 1980 and Margaret Thatcher had just been elected as prime minister. Britain was going into a major recession with millions of people out of work and it was not the best time to start any business.

'I hate that bloody woman and what she stands for,' Bill said, true to his socialist leanings.

'What exactly has she done to you, Bill Lewis?' Mum interjected. 'The country is in a terrible state and needs a change. A woman can do just as well as a man. Thatcher probably will do a better job.'

Bill was not impressed and said nothing. I just grinned listening to the banter, but I was in agreement with Mum on this. The country was in a bad place and we needed a change of leadership to get us out of the rut.

Mum was more like her old feisty self. On her birthday in January, we had a party at the local pub with friends and family to celebrate with her. It was a wonderful night, seeing how happy she was in the company of her dearest and closest.

During this period of time, the banks were not lending because money was so tight due to the recession. Luckily for me, I knew all the hire companies for studios, equipment and the post-production houses. They were more than happy to give me credit to make up for the lack of help from the banks, but I had to be extremely careful with all my cash flow and expenses.

The economy was now in free fall; record sales were dropping and staff at record companies were being made redundant left, right and centre. New younger staff on smaller salaries were being employed in the Artists and Repertoire (A&R) Division of record companies, and they would be responsible for finding new talent to sign up. They were mostly young guys who were expected to understand the current taste in music. I made it my business to start networking with these people as I was the same age as most of them.

In less than six weeks after I started GLO, I had two small budget-acts lined up for video shoots. They were for the Canadian group Martha and the Muffins with their song 'Echo Beach'. The song reached number ten in the charts. The other was for two guys from Liverpool known as OMD, Orchestral Manoeuvres in the Dark, and their song, 'Enola Gay'. This reached number eight in the charts in 1980. The videos were satisfactory but not up to the standard I could say I was happy with. I needed to find good, young creative directors. Mark knew from our conversations that I was getting very frustrated with the quality of people I was encountering; working with music videos required a special kind of director, and I wasn't going to settle for less. This was a serious business and I would only get a few shots from my friendly contacts before I lost credibility and the game would be over.

Into our seventh week, as the phones were ringing nonstop, a woman walked into the office.

'Hello Mark, I was in the area. I just need you to do some research for me,' she said. Mark was brilliant and immediately snapped into acting mode as he saw her coming into the office.

'Hello! Sorry, just wait a second.' He turned to me and said, 'Can you just leave the package by the table over there please? Thank you!' and turned his attention back to the woman in the reception area.

'Sorry, it's a bit crazy today.'

'I didn't think you were very busy in this office, Mark. Is there anything I can do to help? I feel bad asking you to do research for me now.'

'Please don't worry. I'm not normally this busy, but there's a problem with the phones. We've been inundated with calls that aren't for the company. I've made a report to the telephone company so it should be fixed soon.'

'Don't pick up the calls until the lines have been fixed. It's a waste of time.'

Mark left all the phones off the hook so that they would not ring again. Papers were all over the place in the office and as I left, the woman gave me a curious look.

'Who's that young man? Was he using our phones?'

'No, he's only an old friend from university. He was just dropping off a package for me,' Mark replied.

I don't think she believed him. The unexpected visitor was a wake-up call; I had to get my own office. The freebie office period had come to an end. By week eight, I called in a favour from a music friend and managed to get another office; a cheap room in the very fashionable area of Mayfair. Record companies thought my address was very up-market and were impressed. But the fact was, I was living on a month-to-month existence. I even had to sell my car to pay the office rent and the two mortgages.

'What's happened to that snazzy car of yours?' Bill enquired a few times.

'Don't need it anymore, Bill. Much easier just to take public transport or taxis, especially with all the traffic on the roads nowadays.'

I was still using every bit of charm with the contacts I had in order to find work, but I had yet to find a good creative director who understood music. The ones interviewed were mostly from the BBC or ITV and were mainstream or old hat. It was all a bit hit and miss but I managed to secure a television special for a Manchester band, Sad Café. The production gave me a good lump sum and I managed to sign my first lease for an office on the top floor of an old four-storey building in the heart of sleazy Soho. I was surrounded by clip joints, adult bookshops, and signs for promising models. The old building had no lift, and my small single room had three tiny windows overlooking the Berwick Street fruit and vegetable market. I had to share a toilet but had my own small kitchen on the landing. For the first time, I felt like I had arrived. It was winter and I bought an electric fire to warm up the room. This old part of London was very bohemian. I shared the building with sex workers; their little red lights in the windows flaring up when they were open for business. Sometimes their customers would get lost and end up knocking on my office door.

My office rent and the two mortgages were always first to be paid. There wasn't much money left over and I was running up a huge debt on my credit card. I was already renting out the spare rooms in my house to help the situation.

'You aren't working for Mike Mansfield anymore, are you?' Bill asked one day. 'Don't worry, I haven't discussed it with Cathleen.'

We were in the pub enjoying a pint after one of Mum's delicious Sunday roasts.

'How did you find out?' I asked.

'I do notice things, you know. The time you come to visit has changed; the missing car. You don't mention the artists you're working with at the dinner table. Is everything alright? I didn't mention anything to your mother, but I think she is suspects something's amiss.'

'Everything's fine. But yes, I left Mike's company. It was a little tough but all is going well now. You don't have to worry. I'll tell Mum everything when I get home. I just don't want you both to worry, that's all.'

GLO was going to be the vehicle for my countless ideas; I had lots of plans and could see many opportunities ahead of me. Music videos were great, but I also wanted to get into making television shows at the same time. I had one television show which I believed in more than any other. I gave it the working title of 'Where Were You'. The show revolved around music and events for a specific year. Stories of that year would be featured, and in the background, there would be hit songs of that year relating the story or issue profiled.

My pilot show was based on 1967. One of the news stories featured was of John Lennon saying that the Beatles were more famous than Jesus Christ, which did not go down well with the public, especially in America. People were burning Beatles records and memorabilia in the streets to demonstrate their anger.

I needed a presenter and found myself listening to Jeremy Beadle, an unknown presenter on LBC, a talk radio station, and liked his voice and style of presentation. I got in touch with him and we organised to meet in his council flat. When we shook hands, I realised his right hand was smaller than normal. I didn't make any comment but Jeremy sensed my surprise.

'Ah, you've noticed my hand. It's a rare genetic disorder called Poland syndrome,' he said, before I could ask. 'Will it be a problem, do you think?'

'It really doesn't worry me. Your personality and looks are just right for this. There's not much money involved, though.'

'Haha. I'm just hoping something good might come out of the show. Happy to be given a chance to do it. Forget about the money!' he said.

The pilot was done on a shoestring budget with many favours from friends in the industry. We did one long day of filming around several London locations. We had Jeremy talking about The Beatles while walking across the famous zebra crossing on Abbey Road next to the EMI Studios. I directed the shoot with the help of a cameraman friend.

With the pilot, I called David Bell who I knew from my old days at LWT when he was a freelance television director. He was now in a senior management position in the light entertainment department. When we spoke on the telephone, he was helpful and put me in contact with his senior executive producer. When I arrived, he referred to me as the 'messenger boy' which didn't bother me. He was just playing hardball with me.

'I will want LWT to own part of the international television rights for the show and no co-production deal with your company. Also, you have to change the presenter. That deformed hand of his will put people off! He's just not right for television,' he said after watching the pilot.

I never thought it was going to be easy; I was in a weak position with a major television company wanting to keep the international television rights and I had nothing to bargain with.

I decided to keep his disappointing offer under my belt as a fall back. I knew I had to go to America to try and secure some kind of an international television deal. Every year, New York hosted the biggest television sales and marketing event at the Hilton Hotel conference hall which lasted for four days. Looking at my bank statements and knowing I had only two small music promo jobs coming my way, it was going to be make or break time for me.

'You're going to New York?'

'Yes, Mum, I can't work for anybody else. I need to sell my television format idea to an America company. The television companies in the UK are far too old-fashioned.'

'Well then you must go, Gordon. Don't forget, timing

is everything in life. Make that luck work for you.' I recalled these were the very same words Mum told me when I went for my second interview for the messenger boy position.

Mum and Bill had no real idea how close I was to giving up and leaving the UK with its awful state of business and failing economy; more people were out of work every week. I had yet to make any progress in finding a good director and the occasional low-budget videos I was getting wouldn't pay the bills for long. America was looking far more promising and with my credit card approaching its limit, I had just enough left to buy a cheap return ticket to New York. It felt like I was living the old romantic Irish dream; going to America in search of better opportunities. I didn't want to contemplate the possibility of an unsuccessful trip and instead had blind faith in my ability to salvage the situation in America. Mum and Bill were oblivious to my troubles and wished me luck, thinking I was moving up in the world. Little did they know it was my last roll of the dice.

My first two days at the television convention were spent checking out who was who in the business. In my excitement, I did not feel the effects of the time difference between London and New York. I was too busy listening and talking with Americans who I found very different and interesting; they loved to talk which suited me fine.

Soon I had worked out that there were possibly five key senior people that I needed to meet. But getting an appointment with these busy executives proved harder than I thought.

'Can you come back later; he's busy at the moment.' That was the standard reply from all the secretaries. This was a game of networking and I was just hoping for one right person who would say, 'Yes, I like your idea.'

Time was running out and I had only managed to set up three meetings; the first was not too successful and at the second, I received a lukewarm reception. The last appointment was with a man who used to work for the ABC network in a very senior position and had just set up his own company. His secretary asked me to wait a few minutes while she approached her boss, Larry. He was a tall, well-known New York Jewish television executive. I could just see through a gap in the door that he was practicing his golf putting. He had a cigar in his mouth while he was talking to other men in the room. He looked over at me when the secretary spoke to him. I automatically beamed at him.

'You can go in now but be quick, he has another meeting in five minutes,' the secretary informed me as she walked over to the other people in the room.

I walked through the door as confidently as I could.

'Hello, Larry. Thank you for giving me five minutes

of your precious time. I came all the way from London just to see you.'

'Welcome to America, Gordon. I didn't know I was that famous with you Brits.'

'I did my research, Larry. You are just the person for this wonderful television programme idea that I have. The idea is that—' Larry stopped me in my stride with a hand gesture.

'Stop, Gordon, I'm not buying any programmes, I'm only selling them.' I could see he wanted to get back to putting his golf balls with the guys.

'Larry, I know you do buy ideas and programmes for television companies in America. You can't sell something without buying anything' I said with a knowing grin.

I think I got Larry's attention after that.

'What did you say your name was? Gordon Lewis, right?'

'Yes, Gordon Lewis.'

'So, what's your programme about?'

'My idea is to play on people's memories of music and important events that would have influenced or affected them in a particular year. I have here my pilot for the year 1967. Maybe you can remember The Beatles saying they were more famous than Jesus? Well that's in there and The Mamas and the Papas' 'California Dreaming'. It's all featured in the programme, reflecting the hippy movement. If you don't mind, I can put the tape on for you?'

The secretary then walked into the room informing Larry that his next appointment had arrived.

'Tell them to wait,' Larry instructed his secretary. I could see his interest had been stirred.

'You were one of three key people I wanted to do a deal with, Larry.'

'Who are the other two?'

'I can't really say but they've also seen the programme and already voiced their interest. They're keen for an American version featuring more American events and music.'

'I like your enthusiasm Gordon. But I have another meeting lined up. Can you come back tomorrow?'

I walked towards the door which Larry had opened to see me out.

'Okay Larry, but I need to meet early in the morning as I fly back to London in the afternoon.'

He nodded and asked his secretary to put me in the diary for 9am the following day.

I was buzzing with excitement as I left, but I couldn't afford to be too optimistic yet; I still didn't have a deal. I just about managed a hamburger in a diner near the rundown hotel I was staying at.

The next morning, I arrived early at Larry's office.

I was offered a coffee by the secretary while I waited. Larry arrived a little after nine all bright and chirpy.

'Ah, Gordon, you're here already. Come on in and take a seat.' I was excited to see him in such a good and positive mood.

'Let's play the tape.'

I watched Larry's face intently as he watched the tape. It was obvious he was interested.

'Now, I know you're leaving for London today. What did the others say about the programme? You have a deal with anyone?' Larry said after the tape finished.

'Well, one of them is very keen indeed to close the deal but I've given them a deadline 'til this afternoon so that I can see what you have to say first.'

Larry stared at me, trying to work out if I was double-dealing about the other party.

'I'm interested in the show. I like it, really like it. What do you want from the deal? Do you want to work on the American version as a producer? How much are you looking for as a royalty payment for each show?'

This sounded like a dream; I had to control my eagerness and excitement. I laid out the details of the deal to him and finished my demands with the line, 'If you can guarantee me that your lawyer could close the deal with my lawyer in the next two weeks, we can shake on it now.'

'Okay, Gordon,' he said as he offered his big meaty hands to shake on the deal. 'I love you Brits. So straight to the point on what you want!'

'I am actually Irish.'

'Hah! Irish? Never dealt with an Irish Jew before. Fantastic!'

I didn't have the heart to correct him. I had concluded long before that when people thought I was Jewish, I would take it as a compliment and accept it as so.

Leaving Larry's office this time, I was on cloud nine; still pinching myself, not believing what had just happened. I had no real funds to celebrate the event properly and besides, I had to rush off to speak with the lawyer about the deal. It was all very last minute before my flight home that afternoon.

On the plane home, I reflected on my good fortune to meet the right person at the right time; to get what I wanted and needed desperately. I thought my style of doing business seemed to fit America very well. I slept all the way home on the plane, relieved that I had managed to secure something from the trip.

Within three weeks the deal was finalised for six shows, but not without a few calls from Larry telling me I was asking for too much money. It all got sorted amicably and when the contract was finally signed with ABC television, I was ecstatic.

I wanted to share my news with Mum and Bill as this deal meant some real money coming into my business. It truly saved me in more ways than one. I went over to Mum's with a bottle of my favourite tipple, Champagne, to celebrate the deal. They were so happy for me. I put on the music and danced with Mum in the living room. It was truly a happy occasion.

With money now coming in from the States to pay all my bills and expenses, I was free to think about other things in my life. The recession was still biting, and not going away. Larry had already offered me the producer role for my show, and I was tempted by it. I was holding back only because of the uncertainty about Mum's time with us. I was still very mindful that she could suddenly leave us. The doctor's words kept playing in my head.

A few weeks later, I went to see Mum and Bill to sound out the idea of me working in New York. When I arrived, they were watching a classic black and white film, Top Hat, starring their favourite film stars, Fred Astaire and Ginger Rogers. I had grown up watching the film and secretly thought Mum saw herself as Ginger Rogers and maybe Bill as Fred. When the film finished, I dropped the bombshell about working in New York. They were taken by surprise and not sure what to say to begin with.

'Bill, can you make the tea for us, please?' Mum broke the silence.

'If you want to go to America to work, you go. We'll be fine here, so don't you worry about that, okay? But I feel things might pick up soon. I've been listening to the news, I do keep my ears to the ground. Why not wait just a little longer before making a final decision about moving to America?'

Mum was right about a sea of change coming with the economy. The television series got extended to thirteen episodes and then another series of thirteen was commissioned after that. The royalties were brilliant as ABC network's reach of audience was huge in America then. I used part of the money to clear the mortgage for Mum's flat. I wanted them to be secure in their own home no matter what.

Chapter Eleven

Soft cell

Before I went to New York for the television convention, I had been trying out a few new directors, in the hope of finding a more edgy style. In the mix of these was a man called Tim Pope; a tall, skinny and long-haired middle class English guy from London. He was very introverted but showed a lot of promise. He had previously worked in a bank but was now working freelance, showing politicians how to appear on TV. When people met him for the first time, it was difficult to convince them of his talent. They tended to only see his nervous energy and his lazy eye. He made up for this with concepts and ideas that were extremely imaginative and innovative. I decided to use Tim's awkwardness and oddness as a way to get him noticed. RCA Records' marketing director and I had a good working relationship and, it took some convincing, but I persuaded him to let Tim direct two small budget videos.

I had full confidence in Tim's ability, but I needed to surround him with good cameramen, editors and a talented lighting director in order to bring his ideas to life. He was not very assertive with the crew. This was where I came in; you could say I was his right-hand man on the sets, initially.

Around the same time, I met another young guy with original talent; Alex McDowell. He had a small workshop designing record sleeves across the street from my office. Alex wanted to get into film production design but had no experience. I employed him as a set designer to work with Tim. Between them, they came up with countless imaginative ideas.

My big break for music videos came with new acts from the Synthpop movement. Stevo Pearce was one of the hottest new managers; he was only eighteen when I met him, but his stocky build and tough looking face made him look older. This very young, unusual maverick had started out as a DJ at 'Billy's' nightclub in Soho. He had negotiated a deal for his new independent record label, 'Some Bizarre' with a major record company, Phonogram. Stevo had an ability to resonate with the young public. He was a true visionary, signing acts like Soft Cell and Depeche Mode. He was aggressive in the way he spoke and negotiated and I will always remember introducing Tim to Stevo.

'You ain't playin' with my bollocks and floggin' me a dead horse, are you, Gordon?'

'No Stevo, he's really creative. Don't let his awkward exterior influence you. He'll be a star director one day, trust me.'

Steve looked Tim up and down; 'So, Tim, Gordon tells me you're the man who's gonna make me a top class video for Tainted Love.'

'Erm, well yes. I'll try my best.' Tim stuttered nervously.

'You better do more than fucking try! I'll kick the shit out of you if it's a bag of shite. This video is costing me loads, you hear me?'

I was quite certain I saw Tim's self-confidence stand up and leave the building after his first encounter with Stevo's working class bullishness. He really didn't know how to deal with Stevo and was quite scared of him.

Later Tim met Soft Cell, the unlikely duo of Mark Almond and David Bell, to discuss ideas for their first video. They came from the north of England and both loved my down to earth, one room office. Mark was a little camp and chatty; he enjoyed drinking lots of cups of tea while Dave was quiet, reserved, and preferred a pint in the pub.

A few days later, Stevo asked me to join him at the

marketing department of the record company he was signed to. He was ranting and raving about getting a video done; it was apparent to me that the record company was not going to invest the money in Soft Cell. One of the older marketing guys told me when Stevo was out of his office, 'Stevo's passionate about his acts and the music, but he thinks every song his artists produce is going to be a big hit! Making demands for his acts is his job but he can be a real pain in the butt. Let's see where Tainted Love goes in the charts first, then we can talk about a video.'

The record went on to become number one within weeks and there was no time to make the video. Stevo was furious and we were soon back in the marketing department for Soft Cell's follow up single, 'Bedsitter'. This time, he threatened to smash up the record company offices if they didn't sign off the video. His rage was something else.

This video was a turning point for my company. The story of the 'Bedsitter' video was about Mark living in his small bedsit; claustrophobic and spinning about. Mark was dressed to match the wallpaper in the room. This was edited to the driving beat of Dave's keyboard as the visuals took you on a tour of the seedy streets of Soho. Alex's clever production design helped to make the video stand out. The video and lyrics captured what the band was all about. It reached number four in the charts. Within weeks we were working on 'Say Hello, Wave Goodbye' as a follow up which reached number three. Soft Cell's album was pumping out hit after hit and was selling in the millions.

Behind Stevo's aggression was a true passion to achieve the best for his artists, which I had great respect for. He also reminded me of Conner, my old Dublin friend from the hostel; they were both relentlessly confident and showed no fear. Perhaps that's why I always felt as if I understood Stevo.

With the success of the Soft Cell videos, the office phones started ringing with up-and-coming managers and artists wanting to meet me. They all loved the bohemian office and its location, which made the company look cool and edgy. It played well into the aesthetic of the acts emerging on the scene. New artists always liked to see themselves as edgy and different until they became famous and mainstream.

George Michael and Andrew Ridgeley arrived to talk about making Wham's first video, 'Young Guns'. George did most of the talking; he was charismatic and passionate. I already knew George before he got signed up by a small independent record company. My Greek Cypriot gay friends told me how great he was and how he was going to make it big.

Tim unfortunately found George insufferable. George was constantly questioning Tim's camerawork and kept asking for more and more re-takes. I had to step in several times to reassure George all would be fine and calm the situation. Needless to say, the two did not like each other. Though the video and song were a big success, I never worked with George again. However we did meet again, a few years later, when he wanted to buy my house.

The productions were coming in thick and fast, with repeat work from many of the artists. My one room office was getting too small; Betty, who I knew from Mike's office, joined us as my production assistant. My cousin, Ian, joined as bookkeeper and it wasn't long before staff would have to leave the office when clients came in for meetings. We would often end up in pubs and restaurants for less important ones.

I had been in business for just over a year when I decided it was time to buy a building to house the business.

Just before we moved into our new office, I had my first meeting with Paul Weller, formerly of the band Jam, who wanted to talk about a new creative look for his new band, Style Council. Paul was perceived within the music business as rebellious and could be a difficult person to deal with. The fact was he had been making hit records from a young age and knew the music industry very well.

He arrived with Mick Talbot whose girlfriend, Shane, was Betty's best friend. It was Shane who told Paul about my company.

'I hear you're a real diamond, Gordon.' Paul was taking the piss out of me with one of the many words he often used to deride people. Paul picked up such words from his straight-talking father, John, who had been builder at one time but now managed him. I went on to produce thirteen very different videos for him.

Out of the many videos we made, there was one which made GLO infamous. Thanks, or should I say, no thanks, to Stevo who wanted a ground-breaking video for a new song by Soft Cell.

'I want to generate shock waves with this single before the album's released. I want everybody talking about the video and the media fighting to get their hands on a copy.'

I was very intrigued with the pitch, but I really got the message after he played back the song, 'Sex Dwarf'. The lyrics were X-rated and suggestive. Stevo gave Tim a free hand to make the most talked about music video of the time.

The finished video was truly horrifying in a good way, though it was far too sexual and bizarre for its time. We had Mark dragging a dwarf man on a dog lead, wearing nothing but a leather mask, studded collar and jockstrap, with a few naked women scattered around a white room/dungeon. There was raw red meat hanging all over the set. Dave was holding a chainsaw, looking like a psychotic murderer. Everything in the video was completely insane; Mark was even showing off his bottom at one point. The idea was to have lots of naked women in the video, but I was uncomfortable with asking women to do this. I overcame the problem by asking the local Soho transgender and transsexual community, who were more than happy to show off their beautiful bodies and go almost naked for the video. The result was a shocking, scary, X-rated but effective video, depending who you asked!

Initially Stevo managed to keep the video a secret and only showed it to a few very close media people. But his ambition to keep it secret soon came to a halt when the dwarf from the video decided to make extra money and sold a copy of the video to the biggest newspaper, News of The World. They ran a front-page story with photos of S&M, featuring Soft Cell, prostitutes and dwarfs.

The pornography police squad turned up at Stevo's office looking for the tapes, which he didn't have. I had Mark phoning me from a telephone box at 7am that Sunday morning when the paper ran the story; 'Gordon, what the hell is going on? I'm hiding from the media. I can't go home because the police are waiting for me out there. How did that fucking dwarf get hold of a copy of the video?'

I was still in bed and not aware of what had happened. The video was banned by all the television networks and to this day has never been shown. However, many people did get to see it through underground channels and it became a cult classic.

Despite the turbulence of my work life, things were still moving along steadily for Bill and Mum. It was now three years since the doctors confirmed mum had lung cancer. 'Maybe a year, or two at best,' were the words that had haunted me all this time.

Bill took no risks with Mum. She was as quick witted as ever, but not as fast on her feet anymore.

'Cathleen, I'm going out to do the shopping alright? You stay indoors and keep warm. I'll be back soon,' he would say.

'Are you sure you're not just going to visit your second home,' she joked, meaning the pub.

Bill was totally dedicated, like an angel sent to look after Mum. Her home was everything to her; it was her pride and joy. She could still do the cooking but needed help lifting the heavy pots. She would sit in the kitchen and tell Bill what to do.

'Don't overcook the meat, Bill. Let me have a taste. You need to add more salt.'

Bill was enjoying himself, showing Mum what was in each pot as he was cooking; she was still head chef and he, her sous chef.

The only thing they did disagree on was the cleaning of the flat. Mum was very house proud, and Bill was not great at cleaning just the way she liked. She could do the light cleaning but relied on Bill for the heavier stuff like vacuuming.

'This place is so clean you can eat your dinner off the floor,' he would say repeatedly. I did feel sorry for Bill and was looking for a way around this.

In the end, I suggested to Bill that he look for help to clean the flat and I would pay. Bill was very happy with the idea, but Mum was adamant that Bill could do it all. The truth was I wanted to make sure they both had an easier life. In the end a local lady called Yvonne came twice a week to the flat to clean and tidy up. She was terrific and they got on like friends.

Bill loved his local pub, which was less than five minutes away from their flat in New Barnet, north London. He knew everyone there and so did Mum, though she only went there occasionally when I joined Bill.

I would become anxious when the winter flu season came around or if Mum was unwell. I guess I was paranoid. Bill and I would talk about Mum's condition in private, away from home, usually in the pub.

Each year we would celebrate Mum's birthday on the 23rd of January. Bill and I would also celebrate in private, toasting to another year that she was still with us.

'Each day is a bonus,' Bill had said to me many times.

My dream of working in America had not completely left me yet. One Sunday lunch at Mum's she totally surprised me; 'I'm expecting you to go and work in America one of these days.'

'Maybe, but I'm not in any rush now. The business is doing very well here.'

Mum laughed; 'That's a new one from you, not in a rush. Who's pulling whose leg now? I know you better than anyone. I can see it in your face every time an American artist is on the telly, your face lights up.'

My mum was right; I was still fascinated by America. In late 1981, MTV was launched in America and, after a slow start, it took off. However, it relied on British music videos to keep it on the air. It became known as the second British invasion of America. The first invasion was in 1964 with the Beatles, The Dave Clark Five and The Rolling Stones. I was perfectly positioned to take full advantage.

I received a phone call from Elliot Roberts in Los Angeles out of the blue, he was an old-school music manager; a tough heavyweight. On the phone he informed me about his artists. It was not an easy job, looking after big rock and roll personalities such as Tom Petty, Bob Dylan, Eagles, Cars, and Neil Young to name just a few.

Elliot wanted to discuss making videos for Neil Young, having seen Tim's videos for the Pretenders' ('It's a thin line'), Talk Talk's ('It's my Life'), and the Canadian band, Men Without Hats' ('We can Dance') on MTV.

'Neil just loves Tim's work. I love The Cure videos too. Come to LA and make two music videos for us,' he said.

I was interested but I was not going to America on economy tickets.

'What the fuck, Gordon! I'm not paying for business class tickets for you and your team to LA! If you want to travel to LA in business, you pay for it!' 'Look Eliot, I don't need this work. I can do without the jet lag and the stress from a fast turnaround. Whether it's for Neil Young or Jesus Christ; I'm not bothered. It's business travel for my production crew or we don't turn up.'

'I don't have the budget for the business fares!'

'Well, call me back when you do, Elliot,' and I put the phone down on him.

Tim, who was thrilled at the news as he was a big fan of Neil, offered to work without a fee for himself.

'No way am I going to let that happen,' I said.

I already knew you could easily lose your shirt if you

weren't careful in America. The production companies in the UK nicknamed it 'The Graveyard'.

Elliot did ring back saying he had found the budget, but only after shouting down the line, warning me never to put the phone down on him again.

When I met him at his office on Sunset Strip in West Hollywood, his hospitality was second to none and he was nice as pie. However, this man could suddenly turn with the flick of a switch. I thought he must be bi-polar, or was this just the type of personality required to survive in the tough entertainment environment of LA?

Luckily, the videos for Neil turned out great and Elliot was very pleased. More commissions for his other bands ensued, like The Cars. While I was in LA, I was networking with the record companies and managers. Before I knew it, I was travelling constantly to New York and LA with many commissions from that side of the Atlantic. So many, in fact, that I was able to start turning some of them down. Doing business in America just seemed to come naturally to me. The power of MTV was generating massive record sales and in return, the cost of producing music videos went ballistic; my timing was fantastic.

I decided to buy a house and set up office in LA to show I was a serious player and started looking for more directors in the States. I was riding on the crest of a wave but also flying by the seat of my pants.

Looking back, Elliot did me a favour and prepared me for the other American managers who behaved like the mafia. Intimidation and screaming matches being the common way of doing business. They all loved to talk about suing people as if it were a game. I think the drugs were a major contributing factor to their outrageous behaviour. Crazy senseless people fuelled up on drugs and booze. And they were sex mad! At times I felt like I was the odd one out for not participating in their ways.

The only thing that used to worry me were the earthquakes and the possibility of a big one, which the locals said was coming soon. Many nights I jumped out of bed from a mere rumble. After a while, I got used to the minor quakes and reverberations.

Another brilliant director I managed to recruit was Peter Care. He was from Sheffield in the north of England. He was unassuming, very short with a slight build and a mop of black curly hair. He also wore heavy rimmed glasses which dominated most of his face. Again, another talented oddball.

'I don't think I can live in London; everything is so expensive,' He said when I met him for the first time.

'Peter, you need to get real and move to London. Artists won't be coming to your hometown to make their productions.'

As soon as Peter arrived in London I became like his mother, finding accommodation, giving him a loan and setting him up. I soon found him credible artists to work with like Depeche Mode, ABC, and John Lydon, ex-Sex Pistols. I then found him the pure pop act he'd always wanted: Bananarama. They did a cover version of an old song, 'Venus', with a video of the three girls surrounded by young half-naked male dancers. The then-unknown flamboyant choreographer, Bruno Tonioli, played a large part in the production and went on to make a great name for himself in television on Strictly Come Dancing. Bruno was like a lot of creative people who worked on music videos and went on to do other successful things later in life.

Tim was not happy about Peter's arrival, which didn't surprise me. But the truth was, we had too much work. The problem with directors is that they become more demanding as their ego sets in. They start to act like the stars they're working with. I found myself constantly trying to keep a lid on it each time I signed up more directors.

Almost every second week my company was producing a different video, with my roster of directors growing. I was on and off aeroplanes all over the world, loving each and every moment. However, there wasn't a day when I wasn't thinking about Mum and Bill. I felt like I was playing roulette, knowing Bill might one day call with the news that I so desperately never wanted to hear. This was the other side to my life. But I would never talk about my feelings to anybody, instead just pushing them to the back of my mind.

Brian Greene, my old-school friend, married Jackie. By coincidence they ended up buying a house right opposite Mum and Bill. They had a lovely Red Setter called Lady. With both of them working, Bill offered to take Lady out for daily walks and she stayed with Mum and Bill during the day until Brian or Jackie came to collect her. They were a real comfort to me as they kept an eye on Bill and Mum when I wasn't around.

Bill's idea of a walk always included a trip to the local pub, just like he had done with my dog, Brandy, years before. Lady became great company and was almost like a replacement for me while I was away.

Chapter Twelve
The Bubble

I had become addicted to the constant chase; work had become my drug. I was now keen to break into commercials. It was as if I was challenging myself to see if I could make it happen, refusing to hear or accept the word no. For months I tried setting up meetings with advertising agencies but it was a closed shop. After pitching to over thirty agencies, I came across Don White, a man in his late fifties who liked champagne and had great charisma and flair. He was the creative director for McCann Erickson, one of the top advertising agencies. Don took a great shine to me and we would flirt with each other, him wanting to get me into his bed.

'Tonight, we're going to celebrate, Gordon. You're on the go to make Tuborg Lager's new commercial. I've persuaded them to try a very different campaign, more like a music video,' Don informed me while we were having a glass of champagne in a bar in Soho.

'That's fantastic news, Don! Thank you for the opportunity. Cheers!'

'Cheers Gordon! There is a slight downside to this. The budget is very tight, can you make the commercial at minimum cost?'

I didn't take long to consider and offered my hand to shake on it. 'When do we shoot?' I added.

It turned out to be a boozy evening. Don's drunken last words to me as he got into a black taxi were, 'Don't let me down, Gordon. Give me the best ad ever, okay? I'm sticking my neck out for you! If you fuck up, you'll have to go to bed with me! Alright? Ha!'

The Tuborg advert drew on the concept of a human train with music from the Art of Noise. The result was a commercial which went on to win a total of nine gold and silver international awards. The closed doors of the advertising world had suddenly opened as if by magic. The people falling over themselves to get me to make their commercials were the same people who had previously turned me down.

Meanwhile, in America, I was meeting my fair share of outrageous and unconventional people who each deserve their own story in a book. The LA scene was full of oddball individuals and one of the most memorable ones

I met was Noel Marshall. He started out as a Hollywood agent and later became the executive producer for the famous horror film, The Exorcist, where he made a lot of money.

'I'd like to invite you to my safari home this weekend, and I can introduce you to my neighbour, Michael.'

'Michael?' I said.

'Yes, Michael Jackson'

This was all very Hollywood. People were always dropping names into conversation. I was intrigued and went along to the house with Tim, who had just finished a video for Hall and Oates. When we drove up to the house, an hour outside Los Angeles, a beautiful blonde lady appeared to greet us.

'Meet my wife, Tippi Hedren.' We shook hands and exchanged polite conversation. Tippi was famous for making her Alfred Hitchcock film debut working on The Birds. But Noel quietly asked me not to talk about Hitchcock in front of her.

We bid goodbye to Tippi and, accompanied by one of his rangers, we started walking to the safari park. As we walked Noel told me Hitchcock had an unhealthy director's hold on Tippi when making the films. He then started talking about his new film, Roar, which he had not only written but also directed, co-produced and starred in. It also starred Tippi and their children. He referred to the film as his 'baby', as he loved his big cats.

Soon Noel was telling me his life story, and about his broken marriage with Tippi and how they remained friends. It was a very American thing, to hear the life story of someone you've only just met.

We must have walked for over an hour before we encountered two elephants. Then suddenly I spotted the cheetahs running towards us. I almost panicked when I saw the speed at which the cats were moving. I manoeuvred myself behind the ranger. The cheetahs came to a halt when they reached us and started rubbing themselves against Noel and the ranger. Before I knew it, Noel had me lying on the ground playing with them.

'Gordon, they won't hurt you while I'm here,' he reassured me.

'Are you sure?' I asked, freaking out and trying to push the cats away.

'Don't be nervous; they can always sense anxiety.'

I tried to pretend I wasn't scared, but it really wasn't easy. Tim was freaking out even more than me. I breathed a sigh of relief as the cheetahs moved away. That was until some lions made their way over a few minutes later.

'Ah, my best friends are here. I wanted to surprise you, Gordon.' I couldn't have been more surprised if a T-rex had suddenly made an appearance in the safari park. The lions were a lot bigger than the cheetahs, and had a real pong about them. Noel rolled about on the ground playing with them.

'Gordon, look,' Noel said as he put his head inside the mouth of a lion. Just when I thought it couldn't get any stranger! Thoughts were buzzing round my head: What on earth am I doing here with this crazy man and his big cats? He's probably going to feed me to them if I don't do what he wants.

He pushed a lion in my direction. I froze and then fell over when the big cat bumped into me. It carried on rubbing and playing with me like a toy. Noel did not allow the ranger to have a gun and I wondered what he would do if the wild animals suddenly took a disliking to me.

'Can I ride the elephants?' I called out, trying to extract myself from the paws of the lion without agitating it.

'Of course!'

The ranger got me off the ground and onto the back of the elephant. The real reason for this request was to be in a higher, safer place away from anything with teeth and claws!

'We could do a lot together with my LA contacts and connections, and with your talented team of young directors. It would be like a marriage made in heaven!' Sitting on the elephant, I found myself agreeing with everything he was saying.

The next day I enquired about his film, Roar. It had been an accident-ridden production with over seventy members of the cast and crew being injured by Noel's animals. Noel was huge fun but a little too wild for my liking, especially as someone to do business with.

One thing I noticed Americans like to do is to meet over breakfast, lunch or dinner to talk business. I could fill my diary every day if I wanted to, but I was becoming bored with these meetings and was putting on the pounds from all the food and drink. I was also becoming a little indifferent to the LA lifestyle and started to miss London.

One day I got a call from Betty, my PA in the London office, telling me that Jim Beach, Queen's representative, had called. Queen were unique; they always had the final say in the decisions on the creative side and the budgets for their productions, just like David Bowie.

'Gordon, Queen are in Germany and want a music video for the song 'It's a Hard Life'. Can you go to Munich for a meeting with them?' asked Jim.

I was on the next plane out to London and a few days later, flew on to Munich. I had met Freddie when I worked for Mike, and Queen had only been making their way up since then. They had gone on to become a huge international success. On a one to one basis, Freddie was quiet and introverted; not as flamboyant as his stage persona. He loved living in Germany and had made many local artistic friends there. In the video I was going to produce for Queen, he wanted an elaborate party piece with all his friends in Germany featured.

The storyboard for the film was a costume period piece with outlandish designs and over-the-top sets. Freddie was going to be in a bright red tight-fitting costume. He was adding more and more outrageous concepts by the minute! Tim was as straight as they came, but like Freddie became more flamboyant and eccentric as the ideas kept flowing between them.

'Will anybody recognise me when I am all made-up like a red peacock?!' Freddie exclaimed, camping it up. He didn't take himself seriously most of the time and could always laugh at himself. He was full of vigour; a constant chain smoker and swore like there was no tomorrow, but in a funny and good-natured way.

The day before the shoot, the band was out partying in Munich.

'You'll be lucky to see them by lunchtime today. They only got back in the early hours of the morning,' one of the road crew let slip.

John and Brian arrived together in the afternoon. They saw me in the dressing room said, 'Oh, sorry Gordon… we had a bit of a late night. Freddie will be here soon.'

Roger then walked in wearing dark sunglasses, 'Sorry, mate.'

Freddie arrived an hour later. I was used to this; it happened more often than not and was all part of the rock and roll mentality.

I met Paul Prenter, one of the many members of Queen's vast road crew, for the first time. He was dressed in a leather jacket and he had the same kind of look as Freddie, down to the moustache. He was almost a clone of Freddie in every sense except his personality. I was at the urinals when Paul came to stand next to me.

'You're Gordon, right? Irish? I'm Paul, a fellow Irishman,' he said. 'Great set you have out there, just a shame we don't have some treats on the table for the crew.'

I knew exactly what he meant by 'treats'.

'I don't supply drugs on my productions,' I replied firmly as I walked away from the urinals to the washbasin.

'Oh really? And the Pope is not fucking Catholic!'

'Look Paul, I don't do drugs nor supply them, okay?' I reiterated with some annoyance in my voice.

We were the only people in the toilet, and I found him walking right up to me, so close that I couldn't see his moustache anymore.

'Gordon, I don't think you fully appreciate who I am. I look after Freddie; I'm his personal manager. Now do you understand me? Get me what I want, or I can be trouble for you,' he said in his Northern Irish accent.

'Tell you what Paul, why don't you do just that. I am not supplying drugs but I can pull the plug on the production if you'd like, right now.'

He pulled away and laughed, walking out the toilet and slamming the door behind him. He didn't ask me about drugs for the rest of the shoot.

The fact was, for many people drugs were a major part of making music and music videos. Some film productions companies even built drugs into their budgets. Drugs may have been all part of the rock and roll lifestyle, but they were still not something I had any interest in taking or even facilitating.

Over the years I have employed three members of staff, male and female, who were ex-drug addicts and attended weekly rehabilitation meetings while they were in my employment. If they went back on drugs, they knew working for me would be over. They were possibly some of the best staff I have ever employed and I wouldn't want to do anything to risk losing them.

Peter was Freddie's personal assistant and dresser, who had worked for him for many years. They had a fascinating love-hate working relationship. When I arrived at his dressing room during the shoot, Freddie was in a foul mood.

'For fuck's sake, this costume is too fucking tight. Are you trying to kill me? My balls are being crushed.' he screamed.

Peter was sweating away as he tried to get Freddie into his bright red one-piece outfit.

'You must have put on some weight since I measured you last!' he shrieked, as he pulled the costume into position.

'You bitch! I have not put on any weight! Just keep pulling.'

They both broke into fits laughter as Peter gave a huge final tug and the outfit was all in place.

'How do I look?' Freddie asked as he sighed a breath of relief and paraded in front of the mirror.

Before I could reply, Peter pointed to Freddie, 'Your packet is really showing, my dear.'

'Great!' Freddie replied, 'Fuck it, I want the whole world to see it!' He then strutted about, showing everything he had to offer, whilst flicking his hands and clicking his fingers with nervous adrenaline just before his performance.

'Now I'm ready!'

It was a fun and cheerful shoot. At the end of two extremely longs days, the band unexpectedly threw a thank you party after we wrapped at around midnight, to show their appreciation to the cast and crew. Trays of champagne arrived and the party got started! Freddie, while still in costume, began to enjoy himself by throwing food at his German friends. It started a mini food fight and could have become a fully-fledged one if it were not for the arrival of the lady hookers who took centre stage, strutting and flaunting their wares. A little later came Freddie's gay German friends from the leather clubs, most of them in the leather uniforms, almost upstaging the ladies from earlier. The film we had shot was downright subdued compared to the goings on at the party. I left before it got really X-rated, as I was exhausted after four very long days of planning and filming.

Back in Los Angeles, I met Bruce Gowers who had not changed since the first day I had met him at LWT. He was still so modest and without ego, which was rare for a successful film and television director of his calibre. After directing the famous Queen video, he had moved from London to LA to live and work. We talked about old times at the LWT studios. He adored the LA lifestyle and wanted me to join him for a Sunday brunch at a famous showbiz lawyer's home.

I had been to many weekend get-togethers to meet the movers and shakers of the entertainment world and was getting quite bored of them now, but since Bruce invited me, I decided to go to this one. I arrived at a stunning Beverly Hills house, set back from the main road. As we entered the house, it felt like I had just walked into a period film set with loads of old fogies there. They were the Hollywood establishment, conservative and dull in my young eyes. I was more into the pop, rock and roll music scene.

However, the mood picked up when the younger music crowd arrived later on. Seeing so many well-known faces paying homage to the likes of Barbra Streisand, and Liberace who was dressed way over the top for a daytime do, playing the piano. They were considered to be hugely influential in the Hollywood scene. Looking around the gorgeous house I could only see white faces, until I saw Donna Summer. She definitely had presence and was captivating company. She was one of only a few black people there and was standing with her music producer, Giorgio Moroder. Donna was unique, and had sold millions of records as well as working with Barbra Streisand. It generally seemed that black and white people did not mix; this was another unfortunate side to the entertainment business. Working with black American artists like Jermaine Stewart and Terence Trent D'Arby, I began to realise that they had to work twice as hard to succeed against the prejudice of the music industry.

I was surprised by how many guests knew about my production company; this was the golden age for music videos with big budgets and I was happy to cash in on it. My directors were always in the spotlight, which was good for the business, but I didn't care about being in the spotlight myself. That day I was approached by agents and producers about the possibility of getting into feature films, but I did not have the passion for films at that time and was sceptical about the film industry as a whole. Maybe it was because the LA bubble was beginning to wear thin on me. I was feeling jaded with my rock and roll world; Tinseltown and the accompanying lifestyle was losing its sparkle.

It was around this time when I received a call from Bill. Mum has been admitted into hospital again. It was the first time she had been back in hospital since her lung was removed seven years earlier.

I was never great at showing my emotions. In Tinseltown, people are like ants to sugar; you really didn't know who your real friends are. So still, I kept my personal life and my worries about my Mum to myself, all bottled up.

Chapter Thirteen
Appointment with God

It was 1987 and Christmas that year was not a good one. Mum's was still in hospital with pneumonia and Bill and I were prepared for the worst. I was chastising myself for spending too much time in America, chasing what I believed to be my dreams.

Over the years, Bill and I had discretely celebrated the fact that Mum had lived longer than the two years the doctors gave her. We didn't exactly know how she had managed it but we were just very grateful. I never told anyone about my deal with God. But I had, on a few occasions, walked past a church and gone in to light a candle for Mum.

'God, thank you for letting my mum live. Please allow us to have her for a while longer.' I hadn't become religious; it was just my way of dealing with my fear.

After four weeks in the hospital, Mum did make a recovery from the pneumonia, but it had taken a toll on her; she was much slower than before. Bill was older but still very fit for his age, you wouldn't think he was in his late seventies. He was still as smartly dressed as the first day I'd met him with Mum on the O'Connell Bridge in Dublin. It was a long time ago, but I still remembered it as if it were only yesterday. It is perhaps my fondest memory; seeing how happy Mum was, meeting Bill again after almost ten years, and how Bill spoilt me with chocolate that day.

I decided to wind down my LA and London film production company, which employed seven directors. Tim was my first director and I decided to make him an equal partner in the business, which he had always wanted. However, it was not a good commercial idea, creating even more problems for me. I started selling other assets that I had acquired throughout my journey, separate to the production company. I had no idea what I was going to do next.

My friends and family thought that I was having a mid-life crisis as I had quite lost my interest in business. When I was fifteen, all I ever thought of was the entertainment world. I had believed it was going to be my life forever, until now.

'Remember, life can be short, don't waste a day of it.

Money is lovely to have but health and happiness must always come first.' In the past, Mum had always been the first person I spoke to about my troubles. But now I more often found myself looking to Bill and listening to his advice.

The shock of almost losing her for a second time made me take stock of my life and re-evaluate what mattered. I matured through my troubles, and I didn't have to prove anything to myself anymore. I was thirty-three, single and happy doing nothing.

My childhood taught me about hardship, living in open dormitories in Dublin and one-room accommodation in London. I always wanted more; I knew I was insecure. It drove me, believing I never had enough, but I could never talk about my past in order to work through my emotional difficulties of the present. I had been so focused on making a successful business, I had totally ignored my emotional and personal life. I had been lucky in many ways but not in love, perhaps as a consequence of my success driven mentality.

After a few months, Mum was better but still frail. Her mind though, was as sharp as ever and she could be very funny at times. She and Bill would still have little squabbles, like all couples do, but they loved each other more than ever.

I was spending a lot of time with them and decided to

embark on a new project to keep me occupied: designing and building a new house for myself. The project took a lot longer than I thought.

'Mum, I think I'll take a drive to the Algarve in Portugal for some sun and meet up with some friends while I'm there,' I said one day.

'That's a wonderful idea, Gordon; no point waiting for the builders to finish your new house, it looks like it could take a few more months.'

'Yes, but can you do without me? I could be away for a month or so.'

'Don't be silly. I'm fine. Go and enjoy yourself. Just come back in one piece and don't talk to any strangers on the way,' she teased.

This trip was all about me; to find myself and to really appreciate people, things, and places around me. I drove from London to Portugal via France and Spain, stopping in cities, towns and villages along the way.

I was not completely honest with Mum or Bill about my real reason for going to Portugal. Mum had one religious' item from her days in Regina Coeli which she had kept on her bedside table all this time. It was a small, simple medal of the Virgin Mary, which she would hold when she discretely prayed. I had promised God in my deal with him that I would go on a pilgrimage to thank him, if he stuck to his side of the bargain. So, it was payback time.

Fátima is a town eighty-eight miles north of the city of Lisbon and is regarded as one of the holiest places for Catholics. Its fame stems from the apparitions of Our Lady of the Rosary who allegedly appeared to three shepherd children between May and October 1917 on the 13th of each month.

Arriving in Fátima, I saw the magnificent white building of the Basilica. It was a little overwhelming watching the pilgrims slowly making their way to the Basilica on their knees and praying, some seeking forgiveness and some hoping for miracles. There was a great open fire with queues of people throwing walking sticks and other things relating to their illnesses into the flames in the hope it would cure their ailments and disabilities.

I did not kneel but decided to go and light a candle for Mum and have that chat with God in the Basilica. I found the silence inside calming, even with all the movement of people around me. I kept it simple and tried to use humour to make my point without sounding too ridiculous.

'I'm still trying to be that better person I promised you, and to give something back to those less fortunate than me. I'm sorry it took me so many years to come here but I was a little busy.'

I kept looking at the Virgin Mary, wondering if a

miracle would happen there and then, like a tear rolling out of her eye or something. For the next fifteen minutes I remained seated waiting for a sign, but it was in vain. I had one more walk around the plaza before I set off in the direction of the Algarve and its sunny beaches.

An hour into my drive from Fátima, I stopped to give a hitchhiker a lift, thinking it would be nice to have some company and conversation for my long drive. He was a young Portuguese guy in his twenties, with a nice smile. He did not speak any English except for a few words like yes, no and thank you. With gestures and sign language we somehow managed to understand each other. I found myself thinking of Mum's teasing words, 'Don't talk to strangers on the way.'

What started out as a lift, turned into four days of sharing a bed with this stranger. The gestures and sign language got better by the day! My Portuguese was improved with the help of a small pocket dictionary and we both learnt a few words of each other's language. Maybe this is God's gift to me for my visit, I cheekily thought, as I waved my new friend goodbye.

After returning from my trip to Europe, I went to see my private doctor in Harley Street for my yearly check-up.

'How's your mother?' he asked, not that he had ever met her, but I had briefly mentioned her health issues to him previously.

'You know, Philip, I was told to only expect my mum to live for another year or two when the doctors discovered her condition eight years ago.'

'Really?' Phillip said. He was intrigued.

'Yes, they said she had lung cancer. Would you have a look at her x-rays?' I wasn't sure why I suggested this, but I did.

Bill kept all Mum's x-rays in the flat, never expecting to need them again. A week later, after leaving them for Philip to see, I was back at the doctors' surgery. He invited me to take a seat as he took out the x-rays and put them into a light box. He told me that he had looked at the x-rays and had asked for a second opinion from another doctor in his clinic. He had then sought advice from a cancer specialist to confirm their findings.

'I sent them to a specialist to be certain of what the two of us deduced. There is no sign of cancer, Gordon. We don't know how to explain this situation. Perhaps the original doctor got it wrong.'

This didn't make any sense at all. They were the original x-rays of the cancer. Or at least, what the doctors had said was cancer. Had divine intervention taken place; my deal with God? To this day, I could never explain it.

A few days later, I had dinner with Mum and Bill at their home. Mum was smoking a cigarette when I arrived but pretended she wasn't, trying to wave the smoke away with her right hand.

'Do I smell smoke? Is there something burning?'

'Don't be cheeky! Do you smell anything, Bill? The food isn't burnt, is it?'

'No, I can't smell anything,' Bill played along.

'Okay then. Can Bill join me for a drink in the pub before dinner?'

'Take Lady along with you, won't you? She needs a walk.'

At the pub I told Bill about my doctor's findings. He was jubilant at first but within minutes he got very upset. He wanted to take legal action against the hospital and the doctors for their wrong diagnosis all those years ago.

'Mum would only get stressed and upset. Let her carry on enjoying her life, she doesn't need to know what we know. I've had more time to think about this and taking action against the hospital or doctors won't achieve anything.'

Bill kept looking down at Lady, stroking her red coat and thinking about what I'd said. 'Let sleeping dogs lie, is that right, Lady? So, we carry on with our secret?' Bill asked. I nodded.

A few months later I moved into my newly built home. Bill had asked me to meet a few friends of his from the local pub.

Within minutes of my arrival at Mum's, I could tell she wasn't happy about something; 'Bill wants you to meet with his friends at his 'office' and to bring your cheque book along for some bright idea they have.'

She lit up a cigarette. For Mum to smoke in front of me meant she was very annoyed.

'I was only thinking it might be something to keep Gordon busy as he's not doing too much right now,' Bill said.

'He has many things to do, Bill. He's busy enough selling his other businesses and doesn't need you to create extra work for him!' Mum replied icily.

'He'll be doing some good for the local community, Cathleen.'

'Why do you have to meet in the pub?' Mum gave Bill a look to kill. 'If the local boxing club needs help, have the meeting in the club.'

So we did. When we arrived at the boxing club Bill introduced me to three older gentlemen, all of whom were retired, and one who had been a major in the army. They showed me around the club with its leaking roof; the overall facilities were not in good condition.

'This place needs lots of money spent on it, don't you think, Gordon,' Bill said. The three committee members and Bill were looking at me expectantly, hoping I was going to write a cheque.

'I'll try to see what I can do to help raise money. Is there anything you can tell me about the history of the club?' I asked.

They talked about the boxing club as a place for children of local families to learn to box, but more importantly as somewhere to socialise and keep the kids out of trouble. It was indeed a community centre.

'Our Prime Minister, Thatcher, is the local MP and she's an old friend of mine,' said the major.

My ears pricked up. This was just the angle I was looking for.

'Can you invite Margaret Thatcher to the club on the understanding that we're going to raise money for the repairs? If you can, I believe I could do something special to raise money for the club.'

Within less than six weeks, Margaret Thatcher had agreed to come to the club for an hour at 6.30pm on a Tuesday evening for a fund-raising event. I got in touch with friends and business contacts to generate interest. I made it very clear to the groups and individuals that in order to attend and meet the PM, they had to make a generous donation to the boxing club.

On the day of the event, Mum wanted to know if everything was ready for the big night. She was an admirer of the prime minister, believing she was as good as any man at running the country. I had invited her along, but she declined to attend and would rather stay at home. Bill on the other hand wanted to know if he should wear his black or grey suit for the evening.

'I didn't know you were a fan of the prime minister. What's changed, Bill Lewis? You've told me many times you don't like that bloody woman.' Mum teased.

'I'm not going for her. I've helped the boxing club, so why not just turn up and enjoy a drink at the reception. I'm not looking to talk to her but if she does talk to me, I'll be polite,' Bill said very confidently, and Mum just sniggered.

Three hours before the PM was due to arrive at the club, the bomb squad came to check the building and the surrounding area. The IRA were still letting off bombs and the PM was a high-profile target. The invited guests had to arrive one hour before for security checks. It was fascinating to see the number of people wanting to shake hands with Thatcher and be prepared to pay for the privilege. The major congratulated me when I handed over the cheques that evening. At 5.45pm he received the news that Margaret Thatcher was on her way with a police escort. Ten minutes later, the major approached me, 'May I have a quiet word with you, Gordon. A large bomb went off ten minutes ago and now a second bomb has exploded along the route. Margaret's car has had to turn back. She won't be joining us this evening.'

There were lots of disappointed people that evening; families, the CEOs and MDs of companies who had made donations to meet her, but there was nothing we could do about the security alert. When I told Bill the news, he seemed nonchalant about the whole affair.

'Never liked the bloody woman anyway. How about a pint of Guinness at the pub to celebrate the great fundraising event, huh?' he said.

The following year, in January 1990, I decided to throw a big party for Mum's 72nd birthday. Mum did not want a big do, just something quiet with a few close family members and friends at their local pub. But the opposite happened, and she loved it! We all stayed in the pub until late, with a private lock-in after hours. Then it was back to the flat for more drinks and food until the early hours of the morning.

It was a few months after that memorable party that I was in Cyprus with friends on holiday. I had just returned to the hotel from the beach and was looking forward to going out for dinner when the phone rang. Bill spoke with a quiver in his voice before breaking down and sobbing on the other end of the phone. The most feared phone call I had been dreading for years had finally come.

'Gordon, your mum has passed away… I don't know how I can live without her.'

I thought I would be ready for that day, having had

so many false alarms, but nothing ever prepares you for the news of your mother's passing. I took the next flight home to be with Bill.

Bill had always treated me like his own son. As I grew older, he really believed he was my biological father and I would often hear him comment, 'I have a wonderful and loving son; he's one in a million. I'm lucky to have him.' But in fact, I was the lucky one.

After Mum's passing, I knew I couldn't possibly lose Bill too. I believed it was always harder for men to cope on their own and I wasn't sure if Bill would fall into this category, but I wasn't going to sit about and wait to find out.

'Gordon, looking back you did the right thing, not telling her about the cancer. If we did, I think she would have passed sooner,' Bill commented as we sat together for a drink in the pub. Bill's words to me on that day meant more than he could have ever imagined, not that I told him.

'Bill, it's been almost two months since she left us, and Christmas is coming up; let's go away. Just the two of us. How about it?'

Bill had never been to the Far East and he was keen. I quickly booked us a trip to China, Hong Kong, Macau and Thailand, staying in some of the best hotels, with chauffeured cars in each place to show us the sights. We were going to travel in style as I wanted to spoil him.

'Not difficult to spoil you, Bill Lewis. You do know how to enjoy yourself. You won't say no to the finer things in life, will you Bill?' Mum used to tease him, being the true socialist that he was.

The trip did help us to take our minds off Mum for the three weeks, especially over Christmas and New Year.

'China is fascinating, and nobody is wearing western clothes,' Bill said as he kept taking photos.

All the locals were dressed in Mao two-piece green, grey, or navy suits. We dined in a very famous Chinese restaurant serving special dishes that Bill and I had never tasted before. Bill embarrassed me by asking the waiter about each dish that we had just eaten, only to be shocked that it was dog, snake and other funny stuff. Luckily, he asked about them after we had finished eating. Bill was not phased as he washed it all down with the local Chinese beer.

After China, Hong Kong and Macau, we arrived in Bangkok. We ended up of course, like most tourists do, in the famous red-light district.

'The women here can't believe my age. They think I'm fifty not seventy-nine… And I think they fancy me!' Bill said with delight.

Bill was relishing the idea of being fancied and that people thought he looked younger. I'm sure it was a line said to every man who walked into the establishments in the red-light district but he was enjoying himself regardless.

After the Asia holiday, we took a cruise travelling from Southampton to New York. We had a ball and Bill introduced me to the combination of oysters and Guinness. He was always adventurous with food and willing to try anything once. There were still things I could learn from this man.

Bill got the travelling bug after our trips together. He was now wanting to be more independent and started doing his own research on places he wanted to travel to, with or without me joining him. He even started using my credit card, having only ever used cash for all his life.

Bill always took an interest in what I was going to do. 'When are you going back into business? Are you not interested in doing something? It's been two years since you stopped working.'

'I haven't really stopped, Bill. I'm still selling bits off and buying properties instead. It's still work but not as you know it,' I replied.

'Why don't you buy a pub and run it? Great money in that business!' He sounded like an expert, having spent so much money in pubs over the years.

'Haha! Bill, I have no idea how to run a pub. It is just not something I'm interested in.'

Chapter Fourteen

Soho

Out of the blue I received a phone call from an old music friend, Barry Evangeli. I met him when I worked with Mike; he was a promotion person for the record company, known as a Plugger in the industry. We were the same age and he had gone on to set up his own independent record company.

'What are you up to these days, Gordon? Hear you've taken early retirement! How many times have you gone around the world? Knowing you, you must have something in the pipeline.' he enquired.

'Still not sure what I want to do, Barry. I'm not in a hurry though. I'm sure something will catch my attention soon enough.'

'Well, maybe you could help my friend, Colin Peters. He's a well-liked DJ and gay club promoter. He runs a famous gay club, "Bang", the biggest in London. He's got some problems with his lease or some shit like that.'

'I'm not sure I can help. I don't know anything about the gay club market,' I replied.

'Gay or not, a business is a business. And unlike you, Colin isn't very business savvy. Please help him if you can. I'll give him your telephone number.'

I did get a call from Colin. We met at my home; he was all over the place, almost hysterical about his situation.

'I just got kicked out of the club because the lease owner found out I was trying to acquire their lease from the freeholder. Fucking bastard!' he ranted.

On Mondays, Thursdays and Saturdays Colin ran successful gay nights in one of the biggest venues, off Tottenham Court Road in the centre of London. The leaseholder had decided to run the gay nights themselves after finding out what Colin was trying to do.

After almost an hour and going around in circles, it was obvious he needed a good shake up to get him to focus on the crux of his problem.

'Colin, if I were the lease owner, I would have kicked you out too.' Colin was stunned that I didn't agree with him, but he was impressed that I wasn't just saying things to please him.

I decided to try and help Colin as I liked him. We agreed to have an equal partnership, if I helped him kick start his business again. I would strategize and do the deals and legalities, and he would look after the promotion side of the business. In a week, we found new club premises not far from his original venue.

'We don't sign or commit to this new club yet. We take all the door money on the basis that we can deliver a club full of people. They make their money from the bar,' I said to Colin.

He was elated with the deal at first but within days he was calling me up and having long conversations, expressing his doubts and concerns. My strategy was simple: to get him back on the club scene before he lost his following.

'We need to get aggressive and kill off the club nights in your old venue, okay? No time to hesitate, Colin. The longer we wait, the more likely you are to lose this club-night war. So stop doubting and moaning and get your brain working on ideas of how to make the new club look exciting and pull in the crowd!' I snapped, trying to kick Colin into action.

'Oh fuck, Gordon, you're so butch and aggressive… I wouldn't want to get on the wrong side of you! But I love it!'

Colin and I were very different, but our individual skill sets were compatible in a way that delivered success. I think one of the reasons we could work together was because of the fact we had both recently lost our mothers. It connected us in some kind of unspoken way.

We opened the doors within four weeks. Colin threw in everything to make the place special, fresh and happening. The venue oozed style and was way over the top with decorations and special effects. Over the next six weeks, Colin got his club-following back on the Monday and Thursday nights. Our presence was really felt; his old club was losing money they eventually closed their Monday and Thursday nights.

'This is the time to open negotiations with your previous leaseholder. You always wanted to get back to your old venue, right? I'll make a phone call to see if I can do something with the management,' I said.

Colin got nervous as I was about to make the call. 'There are two of them in the management team, one does all the talking and the other is all muscle. They're gangsters, Gordon. Horrible brutes! You know what they would do to people like us.' Colin was camping it up, but he meant what he said.

I was amazed and pleasantly surprised to find that there was a new general manager at the old venue, Jay, a guy I had known from my days working with the singer, Amy Stewart on her videos. We talked about old times and decided to meet up. Colin did not join us as he was still afraid of them.

'Jay, we both know we need each other. Your venue is bleeding money and Colin wants his old club nights back, so let's do a deal for the three nights,' I suggested to Jay.

A deal was struck and signed, and Colin was thrilled. We moved the club nights back to the original venue and the crowd followed suit.

Colin had a large extended family who did not understand business and were suspicious of everything and everybody, including me. They were not too happy that I was Colin's new business partner. They didn't appreciate the work and effort I had put in to get Collin's club nights back, thinking it had just happened by magic. Like a fairy godmother had just come and put everything back to where it was before. I mitigated most of the family's meddling by dealing only with Colin.

I had a trip to New York planned before I met Colin. When the club was up and rolling, I decided to take the trip. Colin had advised me to check out Greenwich Village and gave me a long list the gay venues. I checked out the many bars and nightclubs from leather clubs to strip joints. It really opened my eyes seeing the solidarity of the gay community and its vibrancy.

I found myself walking along the famous Christopher Street in the West Village. In 1969, riots took place between the police and the gay community triggering the start of the gay movement and the fight for lesbian and gay rights in America. From then on, the village became the 'gayest' place on Earth, a mecca in the gay world with its clubs and bars. London did not have an equivalent 'village'. Flying back I kept thinking, maybe one day London could have a gay village of its own.

One Saturday night at the club, sometime after I returned from New York, Colin was very emotional and had a little more to drink than usual. He called me over into a corner for a chat, putting his hand around my shoulder as a sign of affection. He was tearful trying to compose himself, and I just assumed he was overwhelmed with the success of the club until he told me, 'Remember I told about that lump in my neck, and you told me to go see a doctor about it? Well, I did see the doctor and had some tests done… and they… they confirmed to me yesterday…. I have AIDS, Gordon. I am going to die soon.' He crumbled into floods of tears.

I tried to console him and get him to divulge more information about the diagnosis. I couldn't believe what he had just told me. AIDS was the dreaded four-letter word the gay community feared most and it has plagued the community since the 80s. Despite what I said that night, and my efforts to encourage him to fight on, Colin was convinced he would die within weeks. The next time we met, he informed me that he was preparing for his departure and was ready to hand over his share of the business to his brothers.

'Colin, have you sought all advice about the condition. Is there really nothing they can do? I can't lie to you, I can never work with your brothers. We're like chalk and cheese. They can have my shares; I'm not looking for any money,' I said gently.

Colin was saddened but I knew the business wouldn't have worked without him. Within five weeks, Colin had died.

Spending time with Colin had opened my eyes to the gay market and their spending power and habits. On top of that, my New York visit convinced me that London could have a gay village of its own. Bill's suggestion that I buy and run a pub might not be a million miles away from reality. However I was not a pub person and hated cigarette smoke! There were a few gay pubs dotted around parts of London, but they were hidden away from the public. It was almost as if they didn't actually exist; the major brewers were shy about having gay pubs. You could never see the inside these pubs from the street because of their blacked-out windows and the places were mostly run down, had disgusting toilets, with little or no light. They were a place to 'cruise' rather than socialise.

Over the next few months I started plotting and

scheming. I believed bohemian Soho, with its musical history of early performances by the Rolling Stones and David Bowie at the Marquee Club in central London, was the ideal place for my new idea. The Soho sex industry gave it an edge and atmosphere. This was going to be London's gay village, I thought. I wanted to create something completely different, not seen before in London. It was going to be revolutionary, with style and attitude. This was going to be where young gay people could hang out and be proud, rather than hiding away from society. Part of the idea came from Robinson's video, 'Glad to Be Gay' which I produced. He had written the song for the London Gay Pride and I always admired his courage for what he did with his hit song. I had every intention of helping to change the public perception of the gay world.

It was early January 1991, the country was in another deep recession, just like the time I launched my film business almost ten years earlier. However, I saw it as an opportunity with low rents and empty buildings. But I had yet to find the right person to help me put together a team.

Gary Henshaw, a young likeable twenty-six-year-old Irishman, approached me for a job after seeing an ad I posted in the gay newspaper. I was advertising for the new project without giving too much away.

'Gary, tell me about yourself. What have you done?'

'I did have my own small gay bar in Ibiza, Spain, but I ran into problems and decided to come back to London. You're doing something new and I want to be part of it.'

'I'm new to this bar business and looking for the right person with experience who can do stock control, purchasing and manage staff. Can you do that?'

I noticed Gary developed a slight stutter when he was under pressure.

'I can do stock-taking and I know a lot of people in the gay scene.' He had charm but I wasn't totally convinced.

'I want to create a continental style gay bar, something ground-breaking, new and fresh. I know you want to be part of it, Gary, but first you have to take a job in a different gay pub just down the road. Learn all you can about what makes them successful and busy, then come and join me.'

'What, like a spy?'

'Yes.'

Gary laughed. 'Jesus, Mary and Joseph, you're not serious?'

'I'm very serious,' I said, sternly. 'Learn about the suppliers, the sales numbers, what sells best, how the business runs. Whether you end up working for me or not, you'll learn a lot from the experience.'

'What makes you think they'll even hire me?' he

replied.

'They're always short of bar men; they come and go like flies. I'm sure your charm and good looks will get you the job.'

Gary did get a job as a barman, and he acquired valuable skills and knowledge about the gay drinking establishment. I invited him to see my proposed venue, just off Soho Square, to get his feedback.

'It's a bit small, isn't it?' he commented, smiling at the builders who were working nearby.

'A little, but this is a tester for me, Gary. See the huge parking lot at the back. It's going to be named, Village!'

A week or two after visiting the new venue, Gary walked out of the barman job. 'I can't work for that pub owner anymore. He's mad; much worse than you!'

'I hope you've learnt everything we need. Don't expect me to employ you if the information I need is not forthcoming.'

I could become very difficult if I was not getting what I wanted. Each day I would have a list of things I needed to get done. It was a habit I had developed as a producer. Gary was trying hard to remember everything I would ask of him; he never wrote anything down. He was always disorganised, so I bought him a notebook to write down my daily list in and work through it.

Alcohol was my core business. Gary invited the large

drink suppliers for meetings. They expected me to sign a contract for two or three-year for only a small discount, but I was not buying into it. They had the monopoly and were running a cartel at that time; I had to find alternative, smaller suppliers who gave me better discounts and free stock to promote new brands.

Gary's next task was to recruit staff, and he had a great eye for looks. I wanted a young team of boys and girls to reflect the Village's image of youth. The business would be open from 12 noon until 5pm serving food, coffee and alcohol. I was trying to make the downtime during the day work for us. From 5pm onwards no food or coffee would be sold, only alcohol. Beers would be served in bottles rather than pints; it was going to be the new trend in drinking, and a faster way to serve, especially when there was a big crowd. The faster the staff can serve, the better the turnover and client satisfaction.

The bar and lighting was designed by people who had worked for me in the film industry. Mood lighting was installed to make the bar environment completely different and ahead of its time. Large floor-to-ceiling mirrors were placed in well-lit toilets with the first new scented air sprays, timed to go off every fifteen minutes to improve the overall customer experience.

'I want our toilets to be a major talking point for the customers; the cleanest and best kept toilets in the gay pub scene,' I told Gary as we inspected the works on the lavatory.

Gary had a habit of looking in the mirror and adjusting his hair.

'You know, one day I am going to be famous, just like the stars you worked with,' he said.

'Sure you will, but only if the bar is a real success' I said.

I was constantly looking for anything to make the Village bar stand out and to get people talking. Word of mouth was one of the best advertisements in the gay market. I ran a soft marketing campaign for Village West One in the centre of London but deliberately left out the address.

The new staff were all invited to see the bar for the first time. Until then, nobody knew the exact location. I set up targets and bonus schemes, using incentives to get the staff to engage more with each shift. I also introduced small silver trays for tips, which they kept if they smiled and maintained good customer service. This was all about the American-style service I had seen when living in Los Angeles and New York.

'Finally, before we start today, I have one more idea; I want all staff to wear a uniform.' I pulled out the new uniforms which had been designed by Paul, a student from Central Saint Martin's school of design. 'What do you think of the tight white T-shirt with the big V logo, and the black shorts?'

Gary started to snigger when he saw the small black shorts.

'This is no joke. If you don't wish to wear the uniform, you had better leave now.' No one left.

'This will help you to get more tips. I want customers talking about the bar, about the good-looking staff and their hot uniform,' I added.

'We are selling sex?!' Gary quipped.

'Yes, of course!' I said without any hesitation.

'Jesus, Mary and Joseph,' said Gary.

'Let's just call it "eye candy" to make sure the customers remember the Village experience and tell their friends.'

During the staff interviews, I was staggered by the unpleasant stories of many young people who had been told to leave home because they were gay or lesbian.

'When my father found out I was gay, he punched me until I bled and kicked me out of the house,' said one young guy from the north of England.

A very young lesbian lady told me her story. 'I left home in Scotland when I was fifteen because my mother and father could not accept that I was lesbian; they were strong Christians.'

Violence and abuse were common experiences for many of these young people. To work in a gay establishment or gay-friendly environment was therefore very appealing. Some of the new staff were also heterosexual. I wanted an inclusive environment, open to people of all orientations.

Before I could open for business, I needed to have an alcohol licence in place. Getting the right solicitor was important as the major brewers, the old boys' network, would gang up to stop new licences being granted to reduce the competition with their own pubs.

My cousin Dennis had run a pub at one time. He put me in touch with one of his drinking acquaintances, David, who had worked in licensing at the courts for many years. I met David in a north London pub to hear what he had to say and to seek his advice. He was more than helpful.

'Use a barrister rather than just a solicitor, they can argue your case better. Ask for a full licence which allows you to sell everything and refuse the restricted license that they'll offer.'

Courtesy of David, I arrived in court with a stunningly beautiful lady barrister with light blonde hair, exuding sex appeal. We talked about how she was to present my case in court, but she got a little tense when I told her I had already carried out all the building work to the bar.

'Oh, the magistrates won't like the idea that you are pre-empting the license situation. What, you've already hired all the staff ready to start the business?'

'Yes, I didn't think I had done anything wrong, could this be an issue with the licence?' I asked.

Looking around, I saw only male solicitors sitting in the front row of the court to represent the major brewers who controlled the pubs.

'Those gentlemen might object to you getting the licence if your business is very close to their clients' pubs. If they succeed you won't be able to open your business,' said the barrister with a stern face.

I waited to get into the box to give my statement. Three elderly magistrates, two men and a woman, were sitting together looking down at me. My barrister explained that my business was going to be different.

'It is going to be a new continental café-bar concept, not a pub.' My barrister started. She spoke about the improvement to the area, the amount of investment and the jobs that would be created for the young.

After the presentation and deliberation, the magistrates offered us a restricted drinks licence. I could either serve beer and wine but no spirits or serve wine and spirits but no beer. I immediately voiced my refusal to the licence. The magistrates were taken aback, and the barrister asked for permission for me to state the case to them.

'What's the problem, Mr Lewis? You currently do not hold any licence and you haven't proved to us that you can run a licensed business in a lawful manner,' one of the male magistrates said.

'Sir, the bar is aimed at a select group of people, the gay and lesbian community. They will be unhappy if the establishment could not offer what a heterosexual establishment could offer.'

The magistrates looked at each other and started discussing.

'And I have ten, young unemployed men and women ready to start work in this establishment. I want to offer this community a safe environment to socialise and drink,' I added.

All eyes were on my barrister and me, and there were lots of whisperings and grins from the other solicitors who thought it was all very amusing. My barrister turned up the heat, 'Yes, if the homosexual community is not given the same choice of drinks as the heterosexuals, it may be considered to be discriminatory!'

It was all too much for the three magistrates, who said they would need a twenty-minute break to discuss the matter. I ended up walking out of the court with a full licence. The other solicitors representing the brewers were not grinning any more.

Chapter Fifteen

Gay Revolution

We opened the doors of Village West One with eleven young staff members, eight men and three women, on a Thursday night in April 1991. The first two days were fine and nothing special in terms of crowd but from Saturday lunchtime onwards, it just went crazy and the tills were really clinking! From then on, the crowd just grew and grew, word of mouth got around and the takings for each day was constantly going up.

By week four, we had to operate the evenings on a one in, one out policy at the door, enforced by our gay Village security guys dressed in smart black uniform with the V logo. Gary had hired the security guards based on their looks which worried me a little. However, the gay 'Muscle Mary' as they were known – were very professional. There was a guaranteed queue every night from 7pm 'til closing time; I had completely underestimated the interest in the Village idea and how big the market was.

'We need to consider using the back-door access to the car park from the bar to extend the drinking area when it gets really busy from around 6pm,' I suggested to Gary in one of our daily meetings before opening, after seeing how big and constant the queues were to the bar.

'Are you pulling my leg? You don't own the fucking car park, Jesus, Mary and Joseph!'

'I am serious! I just need to get advice from David about getting the space licensed.'

I invited David to the venue the following day. When he arrived at the bar, he found it difficult to concentrate on my questions as his eyes were roaming everywhere.

'Your clientele look so young. You've got some gorgeous looking staff behind the bar, what's his name?' he asked, pointing to a member of staff.

Soon I was back in court with my beautiful barrister and she was able to get the car park area licensed for me. I decided to launch the opening of the outside area with Chinese whispers that Madonna was going to inaugurate the space with a song or two! Just a low key performance…

Seven hundred excited people were pushing their way to the temporary stage built in front of the bar on Hanway Street. She arrived with her four dancers and the Village security surrounded the Queen of Pop as she performed her opening song, 'Vogue'. In the low light and with all the excitement and confusion, it was very hard to tell whether it was Madonna or not. It was in fact the gorgeous lookalike, Steffan, who performed. Gary, however, had the job of dealing with some unhappy customers who had been expecting to see the real Madonna for free, despite her tickets being the most expensive in the world. Nevertheless, with the exception of the few, the rest of the crowd had a fabulous time. The word was definitely out about the new drinking area that summer; the Village bar was the place to be seen with the young and hip crowd. We had to increase the staff to cover the busy seven-days a week operation.

Gary enjoyed talking to the gay media and was inundated with people wanting to work for the Village. He came up with a clever idea to end each evening with a song. The last track played on the jukebox was 'Stand by Your Man,' a country song by Tammy Wynette. This song became a trademark of the bar, with everybody joining in to sing, ending the night.

The bar was a great success with lots of positive feedback, but I also started to receive some very negative comments.

'I don't want any women to serve me, only the guys.'

'You shouldn't let straight people into a gay bar, and

that includes them dykes.'

I began to see that the gay community had its own prejudices.

The complaints mostly came from older men who did not return. The bar became known as the most expensive gay establishment in London with a new younger, stylish clientele who did not frequent the gay pubs with their darkened windows and seedy toilets.

On a busy night, there would be a crowd of about thirty people outside the front of the bar drinking. Inside the bar, on the small ground floor and large basement area, there would be around 130 people. The car park would have another 150.

One Friday night, two plainclothes policemen came to inspect the bar because of the new licence. They wanted to know who the owner was. They were not happy with all the customers drinking outside in the car park and asked me in a very aggressive manner, 'What the fuck are you playing at with all these people drinking in the car park? Are you trying to take the piss?'

I kept my cool. 'Officer, this is my alcohol licence for the car park.' With that, they wished me a good night and told me to increase my security because of the numbers.

Four months after opening, I decided I was going to open my second Village bar, in a much bigger venue in the heart of Soho. There was one person who owned a large number of properties in Soho; Paul Raymond, 'Mr Soho' or 'King of Soho' as he was known. He had a fascinating background. The media liked to play on his early success in entertainment and the sex industry. They saw him as a recluse, only because he did not talk to the media. His real money came from property; investing millions into buying up all kinds of properties in Soho.

I earmarked an enormous three-storey building on the corner of Wardour Street and Brewer Street. It was just across the street from Raymond's 'Madame Jojo's', a transsexual nightclub, where he liked to watch regular live shows after work.

I made a phone call to John James, who I knew from my music industry days. John was married to Raymond's daughter and was fascinated by what I had done with the first bar.

'Sorry Gordon, you know I like your idea, but Mr Raymond thinks your new bar will affect his club opposite. The club is his baby and he doesn't want to see it being killed off by your bar.'

'No, John, my bar won't affect Madame JoJo's. If anything, it will bring even more people to the club!' I tried to explain.

'It's not me you have to convince, Gordon.'

'John, set up a meeting for me and Mr Raymond. Tell him I've met him in the past and he said I could always look him up when I wanted to do business with him.'

'He told you that?'

'Yes!'

As soon as John brought this up with Mr Raymond, I was invited to meet him at his office. I guess he was intrigued.

Mr Raymond seemed much older than I remembered as he leaned back in his comfortable chair behind a large desk. He was dressed immaculately in a dark suit with his long white hair resting on the top of the chair, holding his hands together as if he was about to pray. He invited me to sit by pointing with his hands together to the seat in front of him.

'So, Gordon, you say we have met…'

'Yes, Mr Raymond, many years ago when I was fifteen. I visited the theatre where my father was working for you. You saw me mesmerised by the half-naked ladies on the stage at the time and you teased me about it. We carried on talking and you said I should look you up if I needed your advice or help about doing business. So, here I am!'

'Haha, you have a very good memory, Gordon! I'm getting older, so remind me, who is your father?'

'Bill Lewis, he was a master carpenter for the stage and sets in your theatre.'

'Ah, yes, I think I remember that name. Very lovely

man and a good worker if I remember right. He is well?'

'Yes, he's retired and very well.'

'You want to run a business in one of my sites, I gather?'

'Yes, Mr Raymond, I need to have a second bar in Soho because of the high demand!'

'But my Madame Jojo's...'

'Mr Raymond, trust me, my bar will only bring more people to the area, and your venue will benefit from it.'

'Mmm… you do know the rent is very expensive for such a big site, don't you, Gordon?'

We shook on a deal that very day. Paul Raymond seemed scary and difficult at first but really, he was a pussycat compared to many of the people I had dealt with in the music business.

With the new lease signed, it was full speed ahead to get the new bar, Village Soho, ready for the Christmas business. It meant I had two months to get the bar up and running. It was a repeat of Village West One but was almost four times the size, with three separate and distinct areas for bars within. The big clear windows on the fronts of the venue showed off the modern bar design.

For this bar to work I needed someone with more knowledge about food and beverages than Gary and myself! Going through CVs for a manager, one stood out because an unusual surname: Love, as well as his impressive training and experience in hotels in Switzerland. Mark was a young enthusiastic South African from the corporate world who wanted a new challenge and to work in a gay environment.

Part of my way of working was to try out new things; it's just part of my quirky personality. So I sent a sample of Mark's handwriting away to be analysed, without telling him. The results of the analysis were very positive. I later told him about the handwriting analysis and he was very much amused. I sent him to the West One bar to write a detailed report of what he saw as the positives and negatives; what was working and what wasn't.

'Just be honest and don't let anyone who works there know what you're doing,' I said.

'Okay, but do I get paid for this?'

'Yes, and a job offer if I'm impressed with your report!'

Mark was as impressive as his CV and the report was very revealing. He had been to the bar at different times of the day and had worked out which of the staff were helping themselves to the tills and giving away free drinks to their friends. He believed food wastage was far too high and had strong ideas about how the business could be improved.

'I would like to offer you an assistant manager job immediately. The manager's job will follow at Village

Soho when it opens. First, I want you to do a complete review of everything we're doing. Can you start with an alcohol stock take?' Mark jumped right into action.

Gary arrived a few hours later and I also instructed him to do a stock take.

'Jesus, Gordon. I just did one two days ago!' Gary complained.

'Just get on with it, Gary, okay?'

The difference between the two stock takes was tremendous. Gary's stock take was way out, not noticing the missing alcohol.

Mark was what you would call a system operations person and very efficient. With building contractors working on the new site, Mark always carried around a clipboard with his list of things to do. This led to endless jokes from Gary who gave Mark the nickname 'Clipboard' from his first day on the job. Mark did not take any offence and gave back as good as he got with an even more acidic tongue. He christened Gary, 'Hairspray Henshaw', reflecting the fact that he always had stiff moulded hair, held together with hairspray, and was constantly looking in the mirror.

Interviewing new staff was fascinating. Gary always went for good looks, great physiques and had a soft spot for the Brazilians and Italians; Mark was looking for people with food, beverage and bar experience. All the salaries were equal for men and women, which was original for its time. With so many good-looking young staff wanting to work for the Village, I soon had a new problem: Gary was using his place of work like a dating agency. This led me to create a new rule for all the managers.

'If I hear of any of you dating a junior member of staff, you will be out of a job.'

Next to the Village Soho was Tisbury Court, a small but busy side street where many striptease bars operated. There were always male pimps hanging around door entrances touting for business.

With bright neon lights flashing away day and night, it was an attractive sight, almost like a stage set. As part of our ethos of being accessible and visible to the general public, I got rid of all the coverings over the windows and let the natural light in during the day with French doors opening onto the side street so you could see all the activities going on there.

The next day I was confronted on the side street by one of the pimps; 'Hey mate, you work in there? Is it true this is going to be a poof's paradise for all the fairies?'

I just smiled back. 'Yes, you have it in one, mate.'

He shouted back, 'Cover up those windows and doors, won't you?! Don't want all them dirty queers looking at us as we work. It'll affect our business, and we don't want that, do we? If you don't play ball, the place could get burnt down… you know what I mean?'

I stopped and stared at him, quite calmly, 'Thank you for letting me know that, mate. I'll inform the new Irish owners about this. You do realise they'll bomb every sex shop and girlie bar in this area when they hear about it, don't you?'

The IRA still had bombs going off in London at that time.

He stuttered as he replied, 'Hey, it's not me who wants the place on fire… I'm only repeating what I've heard other people say.'

'Well, you go tell them who owns this place, and everyone can just get on with their own business! Alright?!' I said, and then turned on my heels and walked away.

The last time I used the IRA in this manner was in New York. I was dealing with a well-known New York rock manager who was pushing his luck and spouting off about his Italian Mafia background and family connections. 'My family are Italian, and I expect only the best produced video from you, you understand? I have never spent so much money on making a music video?'

He did have one of the hottest American duos at the time, but I did not take kindly to his intimidating manner. I decided to give him a dose of his own bullshit and got a little theatrical.

'You know what, we have so much in common. All my

brothers and most of my family are in the IRA. They like to bomb and kill people too!' I lied.

He laughed, unsure of whether I was joking or not. No bullets flew nor bombs went off, and he surprised me by sending my director back to London on a concord flight at his expense!

Village Soho was ready to open on time, with much effort on my part to push things along. I started to get a nickname, 'Slave-driver' which was just one of many nicknames I'd been given over the years. For its opening night, I planned the biggest and most glamorous private party Soho has ever seen. Invites went out to gay and gay-friendly celebrities including the pop stars of the time, the Pet Shop Boys and Andy Bell from Erasure who reminded me of the late Colin Peters with his good looks and sense of humour, as well as gay club promoters like Jeremy Joseph and Laurence Malice from Trade. The sisters Kylie and Dannii Minogue were going to be the icing on the cake. The gay media talked about this being the potential start of a gay revolution in Soho, with more business to follow. It felt like my dream of creating a gay village in London was going to be possible.

However just before the VIP guests started to arrive, two of our security guys, dressed in black with the Village logo on their jackets, came looking for me.

'Some strange old guy dressed in a black Crombie

coat with long white hair is asking for you. He has no VIP invite and was not on the guest list.'

'Shit! Where is he now?' I asked.

'Waiting outside the café bar door.'

I hurried to the door entrance and invited Mr Raymond in. He was most charming and amused.

'Sorry, Gordon, I dropped in unannounced. Would you mind if I had a look around your new bar before the party starts? I won't stay long.'

We walked around the three bar areas and he was pleased with what he saw. He asked if he could have a drink in the café bar area, which he liked very much. When the young bar tender served him his drink, he insisted on paying for it, even though I was adamant it was on me.

'Please, Gordon, you must let me pay as you are going to be owing me a lot of rent soon. See it as good luck.'

He pulled out the biggest note and put it on the silver tray and told the bar tender to keep the change.

We sat there and chatted for about ten minutes before his black Rolls Royce pulled up outside. He wished me well as he got into the back of the car and it drove off.

Village Soho was an overnight success, attracting even more young gay people to hang out in Soho. Fashionistas, models and pop stars like Jimmy Somerville or Mark Almond would pop in for their lunch or a cappuccino during the day, as well as drinks in the evening. It soon became a place for mingling and meeting people; a place to see and to be seen.

This was before social media and gay dating sites. It was like entering a sweet shop of treats with so many people wanting to hang out and say, 'We're gay and proud of it.' It was revolutionary as a place for the young gay people to invite their straight friends to and be confident in being there. Very soon the Village bars were the busiest drinking establishments in all of Soho.

I always knew alcohol was going to be a money-spinner, but it was the popularity of the affordable cappuccino with a biscuit that surprised me; this was well before the coffee revolution started. Food sales came a poor third in the pecking order.

During and after the opening of the bars, I had less free time to travel with Bill, but I did find some short breaks we could do together. Bill loved the lifestyle on the cruise ships after our marvellous experience on Cunard's QE2 cruise liner to New York. He had been bitten by the travel bug and was soon on holidays all over the world. His next cruise was to the West Indies, a place he had always wanted to go. This time all on his own.

Bill had always been a cash man from the first time I met him as a boy. I had to persuade him not to take large amounts of cash when travelling. My credit card became his new best friend and I enjoyed teasing him about it. The travel reminded Bill there was still life after Mum and he had started to enjoy his new independence.

Bill asked if I would join him on a trip to Dublin one day. 'Fancy a trip to Dublin with me? I've not been back to the old country for years. Must have changed somewhat.'

'Sure, I'll join you, but what do you actually have in mind to do there, Bill?'

'I'd just like to take a trip down memory lane.'

I wasn't entirely sure if he was telling me the whole truth. Bill did not really have many fond memories of Dublin because of the bigotry he had encountered from his mother and sisters when he wanted to marry my mum. I booked a flight and we stayed three nights at the Shelbourne Hotel for old time's sake.

This trip was really to see family and friends. Bill was now the only one left of his eight brothers and sisters. He was soon enjoying the fuss people were making of him. I could see he was happy to be in Dublin again.

'Bill, you look great. How old are you now? You don't look your age.' For a man in his mid-eighties, he was in good health and indeed did not look his age.

He liked to hear the glowing comments. Mum was right about his vanity, but he never let it get to his head, partly because Mum had always been there to remind him.

We went off to Maynooth to meet my Aunt Lilly and her family. We all ended up in the pubs; some things never change.

The next morning, I joined Bill at the breakfast table by the large hotel window over-looking St Stephen's Green.

'Good morning, Bill. Slept well?'

'Like a baby, Gordon. It's very comfortable here.'

'So, have you ordered?'

'A full Irish breakfast!' Bill replied with a cheeky smile

'I was expecting you to say that!'

'Am I that predictable?'

'I know you Bill… I bet you ordered a pint of Guinness as well!'

'Haha, you know me very well indeed, and yes, I guess I am predictable. Will you join me for a pint of the black nectar? We are on holiday after all, go on.'

We had two pints each that morning with breakfast and we did the same again the next day!

On our last night in Dublin, we had drinks at the hotel bar. Bill was surrounded by relatives and friends and looked dapper from head to toe. He was buying drinks with his credit card and I could see he was getting quite merry. It soon became a typical Irish evening of laughter, singing and drinking.

'What a great night, Gordon. Do you remember when you, Cathleen and I met on the O'Connell Bridge? You were only…' He stopped mid-sentence and looked at me with his eyes half-closed and his body slightly swaying back and forth while holding onto his pint of Guinness. I sensed what he was going to say next, but didn't continue. He did not break the unwritten rule that existed between the three of us; not bringing up the Dublin past.

I went to bed happy, knowing Bill had a fantastic time and saw Ireland in a different light. Dublin was changing for the better. Young people wanted more openness and the Catholic Church did not have the same level of influence over people as before.

That night I had the most vivid dream. In it, I found myself getting into a car outside the hotel. The driver asked, 'Are you ready for the long drive to Cork, Mr Lewis?' I was in the back and soon I found myself nodding off while watching the Irish countryside in virtual silence. The next thing I knew, I was in some kind of misty forest, and the car arrived outside a large house with a drive and open gates, in an affluent area of Cork. The driver spoke suddenly.

'Ready to meet your father for the first time? That's John Sullivan over there with the little girl.'

The little girl was running around, screaming with laughter and shouting out 'Grandad' as the man ran after her.

I looked out of the window and saw the shadow of an old man walking towards me holding the little girl. I froze.

'Hello, Gordon. I'm John Sullivan, your father. Are you looking for me?' the man said.

In the dream I wanted so desperately to see his face and to know what he looked like. But I could only see my own face and my own expressions, no matter how hard I strained my eyes to see. I wanted to ask him why he abandoned my mother and me, but just as I was about to speak, to my dismay, I saw Bill walking towards the car with a very disappointed and sad face. It was a horrifying moment; I felt ashamed having gone to meet my biological father when I knew in my heart of hearts that Bill really was my true father. It was he who had cared for and loved me and my Mum. Just as Bill turned to walk away, I tried to get out of the car to hold him close to me and tell him how I really felt. Instead I found myself falling and then jolting awake in a sweat. The dream was so vivid; it kept playing in my head all night. I could not get back to sleep.

In the morning Bill and I had breakfast together again and I made no mention of the dream I had the night before. I was watching Bill thoughtfully when he suddenly broke the silence; 'Gordon, I am so lucky to have you as my son. You have given Cathleen and me so much joy and more than we could have ever imagined. You know I am very proud of you, don't you?'

It was out of the norm for him to be expressing his feelings quite so openly. For once, I was stuck for words. Bill had caught me off guard and what he said was made much more poignant by my dream.

He broke eye contact with me and looked out the window, sighing, 'I remember when you were young and you used to ask me why I never bought us a place to live in.' His voice wobbled slightly. 'Seeing the joy you brought your mum when you got us the house, well it's the happiest I ever saw her. I should have done the right thing for you both all those years ago.' He looked at me and his eyes were filled with regret.

'Bill, you did your best,' I insisted. 'Mum wasn't unhappy in the flats. You gave us a new start and a home when we needed it most. I wouldn't have made it to where I am today without you. You gave us hope in a dire situation, Bill, and Mum and I will always be grateful for that.'

Bill nodded thoughtfully and returned to his breakfast, allowing us both a second to compose ourselves.

'Knowing you, I expect you'll sell the bar business when you get bored, right?' he said through a mouthful of bacon, with his Clark Gable smile. A smile I will never forget.

Three months later, Bill had a major heart attack and passed away. It was sudden, and I gave him an Irish farewell, just the way he would have wanted. I can honestly say Bill had lived his later years to the full. Whenever Jackie and Brian took Lady for her daily walk after Bill's passing, she would always pull them in the direction of his flat across the road.

I decided to sell the flat I had bought Mum and Bill, as there were just too many memories there. A year later, the young couple who bought it were removing the wardrobes in the bedroom and found a hidden area built into the back. Jackie phoned me with excitement in her squeaky Midlands accent, 'There was a secret compartment behind the wardrobes, Gordon! There were a lot of documents in a large brown envelope. The couple gave it to me to give to you.'

It was only when I got home that I opened the envelope. It contained legal papers, such as Bill and Mum's marriage certificate in London, a local newspaper cutting of the announcement placed by Bill of Mum's death, documents of my adoption by Bill from the British Juvenile courts and my earlier Irish birth certificate, where the space for the father's name was left blank.

As the years passed, Bill and Mum believed I had forgotten my Dublin past because we never talked about it. The truth was, it was all just locked away at the back of my mind like the hidden documents in the wardrobe.

A few months after Bill passed away, Jackie told me their dog, Lady, had also died of old age.

Chapter Sixteen

Sultan of Soho

After losing Bill, I threw myself into expanding the Village idea for Soho. Work was my way of dealing with the loss. With the two busy bars, I turned my mind to the gay club scene, knowing I could move my customers from my bars into a nightclub. I turned to my old friend, Mark Wardel, also known as 'Trademark', for some help.

Mark had worked on many storyboards for my music productions. He was a creative guy and you never knew what he might conjure up. I wanted to use his artwork to get me maximum media attention and to get people talking. He did exactly that and came up with some German inspired artwork showing young good-looking guys grouped together on a hilltop wearing uniforms, almost like those worn by Hitler Youth, with V logo flags in the background. The artwork was a little controversial but so eye catching; it got the media's attention alright and plenty of free publicity. We called the new club night event, Village Youth.

Part of the new club idea was to showcase up-and-coming live music acts on stage each week. Gary was over the moon about my new venture and wanted to be the frontman for booking acts for the club. This was his moment to be famous; his dream, meeting the stars. But I had to restrain him when he came back to me with ludicrously high costs for the acts.

'Tell the record companies we'll help their act to break into the gay market. We can't pay these silly sums of money for a club night! Find the gay managers, they always know how important the gay market is to the music industry.'

After the initial reprimand and lecture, Gary did find great acts within the budget, every week. Take That was one of the first new acts booked to appear, with Bonnie Tyler and Lisa Stansfield to name a few. Advertisements were placed in the media using Mark's artwork and there was a real buzz in the build-up to the launch of the club.

The venue was just around the corner from Village Soho Bar and had once been a church, which the gay market found rather ironic. The youths came in droves and they dressed to kill. The guest list was always inundated with pop stars, models, including the first openly gay football star, Justin Fashanu.

Coming out as gay is never easy for anybody, but for a black footballer it took exceptionally great courage. He had been subjected to malicious jibes from fellow players and abuse from football fans. He became one of the many regulars.

Running a successful business in Soho, I lost count of the times I was asked, 'Did you have to pay any kind of protection money?' There were always rumours that local businesses were approached by gangs for protection money. I am happy to say I was never approached. I often wondered if my chat with the pimp on the side street went viral in the Soho community…

When the word got out that I was planning to open a third bar in Soho called 'The Yard', the gossipers said I had lost my way.

'He's crazy to open a third bar, Soho just can't take it!' they said.

I believed the more the merrier. I was always hoping others would join me to make Soho the gay village that I had envisioned. Only by having more gay businesses in Soho would this happen.

The Yard was in a run-down property set in a courtyard next to Village Soho; it was like a hidden gem. To me the old brick walls and the wooden floors were part of my idea of developing a very different kind of bar with a more bohemian style. It would be known as 'Yard Bars'. Major works were carried out and the place was jazzed up with old large mirrors and old leather furniture. It had a fantastic open area for drinking which was key to the success of the business. I decided to introduce 'Show Time' at the Yard Bars every Sunday night. Our acts featured the most famous drag queen at the time, Lily Savage, alias Paul O'Grady, and Graham Norton.

Soon other gay businesses began to open: hairdressers serving the gay market, tanning shops, restaurants and gay sex shops that sold more than the usual paraphernalia, included clothing, greeting cards and accessories. The gay media started talking about the new 'gay village' in Soho. I found myself being asked for advice about starting up businesses there. Other new gay bars soon arrived, in competition with mine, but I always believed there was enough business for everyone and it never bothered me. Most customers didn't know me or what I looked like. I liked the staff to be the face of the business and Gary adored the limelight, which suited me just fine.

London quickly became the gay capital of Europe; the word spread all over the world about the happening

Soho scene and the international tourists arrived in huge numbers, wanting to capture the atmosphere and the excitement of the place. Soho had arrived.

In my first two years at the Village, I went along to the Gay Pride events. The famous Gay Pride march happened every year in central London, followed by a big party held in one of the London parks. It was a costly business staging such a major event with a huge number of people involved. It was seen as a great celebration with appearances from pop stars and celebrities, and entrance to the party was free. The Gay Pride organisers had many principles and worthy intentions, but the event was poorly run and they always lost money. People and companies did not get paid as a consequence.

I was invited to a meeting with the Pride organisation to see if I wanted to get involved to help them. I was seen to be a commercial operator because of my background. I gave them my feedback, their shocked faces said it all.

'Make everyone pay to get into the event. Unless they're unemployed or have a disability. The gay community can afford it. If they can travel, party, drink and take drugs, then they can pay an entrance fee of some kind to ensure the event doesn't lose money,' I said.

You could have cut the atmosphere with a knife. Gary didn't say anything, he was too busy looking down at the floor until we walked out of the meeting.

'What did I say wrong? I was honest,' I replied.

'Yes, but it was so black and white the way you said it, Jesus, Mary and Joseph.'

The Centre Point Charity in Soho did amazing work for young homeless people arriving in London. I got to know about the centre when we opened the first bar. They approached me because many of the young homeless teenagers in the centre were gay and had been kicked out of their homes when they 'came out' to their families. I had a keen interest in this Soho charity, having grown up in a hostel myself, I quite understood what it was like. It started with simple collections of money at the doors of the bars.

Then I planned an all-day charity event for Centre Point Charity at the famous Queensway ice rink in Bayswater called, 'Queens on Ice.'

The name was very much in keeping with the venue and everybody had to donate to gain entrance for the day.

It was that Saturday lunchtime at the Queensway ice rink event that I met my future partner. I knew the first time I laid eyes on him; he was the one.

'Sorry, but can you help me to learn how to skate? Never been on ice before,' was my opening line when he was next to me. He kindly obliged with a smile and offered me his hand to help me along. He told me to steady my stance while showing me how to move my skates in a certain motion to enable me to go forwards.

I continued holding onto his shoulder to steady myself and play-acted the part until some more conversation was struck. Later Gary called out my name to get my attention.

'Are you part of the organisation of this event?' he asked.

'Yes, I'm Gordon,' I smiled.

'I'm Yew Weng. Nice to meet you'

'I just need to see what he wants, but I'll be back, okay?'

'Okay.'

I attended to Gary as quickly as possible and returned to the rink, but I couldn't see the man anywhere. I regretted not taking his number before I left. As I walked past the café area, I spotted him.

'Hi, I thought I'd lost you when I didn't see you on the rink,' I said.

'Oh, I just got a little tired,' he replied.

'Can I get you a drink? I'm going to get myself a beer.'

'No thanks, I just had a coffee. You go ahead.'

'So, what do you do?'

'Well, I was a chartered quantity surveyor until a few months ago, when I gave up my job to pursue dance.'

'Dance? Wow, that's great. I'm looking for dancers all the time for the club… though I don't think that's the kind of dancing you're looking to do.'

'Haha. What kind of dancing are you talking about? Ideally, I am hoping to do modern dance for a group or West End show, but it is very hard to get into. Having said that, I have a show with a small troupe in Sadler's Wells for three nights starting in a couple of weeks' time.'

'Wow, that's fantastic. Tell me how I can get tickets for it. I'd like to go!'

We spent the whole time talking; he had come from Malaysia to do his university degree and then stayed on after getting a job in a large quantity surveying firm. He was a little taken aback that I owned the bars and clubs, not necessarily in a good way I think. He must have been worried about what kind of person I was to be involved in nightclub and bars, surrounded by so many good-looking customers and staff. Instead I talked about my music and television days, which he found very interesting.

We exchanged numbers and two weeks later I turned up for his show in Sadler's Wells. He was dazzling and had such presence on stage. It took Yew Weng months to agree to have a date with me. You could say he was suspicious of me, but he was also busy embarking on a new challenge in dance. When we did get together, it was like magic. He moved in a month later and that was that. As I write this, it has been twenty-seven years since we got together. Looking back, I see the Soho charity event as good karma. Sometimes life can deal us a good hand and it's down to us to take hold of the situation.

Being all loved up, and with the business running well, I felt the time had arrived for Soho to have its own yearly get-together to promote businesses in the area and the LGBT community as a whole. I invited every Soho business, gay and straight, for a meeting to try to get this going. It was a very slow start as many businesses were sceptical of my intentions so in the end, I decided to just get on with the event, come what may!

After a few positive conversations with Steve and George at The Compton's gay pub in Soho, we decided to see if we could make a little bit of history! Contact was made with the police and the local councillors; Steve approached the local church to use their park, St Anne's Gardens for the event. We were on the go with a charity event known as The Soho Pink Weekend! It doesn't take much to get a gay party going when the gay media gets involved.

The first Soho Pink Weekend started on a warm Friday evening in the summer of 1993, with each Soho business having to do something for their charity and customers. The Village Soho invited the royals, Princess

Diana and Prince Charles, for the cutting of the red ribbon ceremony to signify the start of the Soho Pink Weekend. They arrived in a black Rolls Royce as cameras flashed everywhere and the crowd outside grew so fast the traffic in Soho came to a standstill.

Excited onlookers couldn't believe the royals were arriving and they surrounded their car and the main bar entrance, with the Village security trying to hold them back. My head of security was pleading with me to get the 'royals' (lookalikes of course!) back in the Roll Royce and away from the bar as the crowd was just unmanageable.

That next day, the party carried on in the street with a carnival atmosphere in the streets of Soho. The whole weekend was the busiest Soho had ever seen. Glamorous drag queens turned up in droves as they always liked an occasion to dress up. Paul Raymond's legendary Madame JoJo's staff joined in the fun on the streets and embraced the occasion. The weekend's very hot weather encouraged the gay community to wear very little and Village Youth put on a special Saturday Soho Weekend club night.

On the Sunday afternoon, the parade started at one end of Old Compton Street and marched down to Village Soho at the other end and on into St Anne's

Gardens. With a minimum donation for entrance to the garden, much was raised for Centre Point that day. In the parade were the lesbian pipers and drummers all dressed in matching uniforms. They created a breathtaking atmosphere which started with the drummers making rousing sounds to get the party going, followed by the pipers. More than twenty drag queens, dressed to the nines for the special occasion, followed the Village staff in their uniforms as they waved the Village flags. Compton's staff came next, dressed in leather outfits and little else, followed by more gay business staff who were also dressed up. The gay community looked on waving and blowing whistles and making lots of noise. After about twenty minutes the parade finished at the park.

Inside the park a small stage had been erected and the event started with a lesbian and gay dog show, voted by the audience's cheers. Then came the beauty competition to elect Mr Pink Soho, as some good-looking guys competed in swimwear for the title. The programme was filled with comedians and pop stars performing right through into the night.

The police had closed off the streets of Soho and local bobbies got into the party mood. Later that day a senior policeman, in charge of overseeing the weekend's event, approached me to say how good-natured it had been and that he would support the event the following year if we applied again. It was fantastic fun and all my hard work organising it paid off. Over the years the event just got bigger and busier.

Bill predicted I would sell the Soho businesses, and he was right. For me, it was always about the challenge. I had set out to create a London gay village and my Soho adventure, after four years, was now over. I was given quite a few different nicknames along the way, but the one I liked best was, 'The Sultan of Soho.'

www.secretchild.com

ACKNOWLEDGEMENTS

I would like to say thank you yet again to Yew Weng for his tremendous help and patience. Without his guidance and support this second book would not be possible.

Also a big thank you to Olivia Ballington (Liv) from Sheffield!